REGULATING SEX FOR SALE

Prostitution, policy reform
and the UK

Edited by Jo Phoenix

LEARNING
RESOURCES
CENTRE

HAVERING
COLLEGE

This edition published in Great Britain in 2009 by

The Policy Press
University of Bristol
Fourth Floor
Beacon House
Queen's Road
Bristol BS8 1QU
UK

Tel +44 (0)117 331 4054
Fax +44 (0)117 331 4093
e-mail tpp-info@bristol.ac.uk
www.policypress.co.uk

North American office:
The Policy Press
c/o International Specialized Books Services (ISBS)
920 NE 58th Avenue, Suite 300
Portland, OR 97213-3786, USA
Tel +1 503 287 3093
Fax +1 503 280 8832
e-mail info@isbs.com

British Library Cataloguing in Publication Data
A catalogue record for this book is available from the British Library.

Library of Congress Cataloging-in-Publication Data
A catalog record for this book has been requested.

ISBN 978 1 84742 105 0 paperback
ISBN 978 1 84742 106 7 hardcover

Cover design by Qube Design Associates, Bristol.
Printed and bound in Great Britain by MPG Books Group

Contents

List of figures, tables and boxes

Figures

Tables

Box

Acknowledgements

This book started life as a special edition of *Community Safety Journal*, guest edited by Jenny Pearce and Jo Phoenix. The two editors brought together a series of authors who could offer some insights into the implications for community safety of the proposals to deal with prostitution put forward by New Labour in 2006 and contained in *A Coordinated Prostitution Strategy and a summary of responses to 'Paying the Price'* (Home Office, 2006). Most of the chapters within this book were presented and published in that journal, albeit as much shorter pieces written for the specific readership of that journal, that is, largely police and other criminal justice practitioners. Although each of us was very happy with the final product of that collaborative effort, we also felt that there was a need to reflect more deeply on the profound policy changes that have taken place and to ask broader questions about their implications for specific constituencies of sex workers, about the processes of consultation and the assumptions made by government about sex work, and in doing so to pose the question of what, if anything, is new or different about these policy changes.

Inevitably, many debts have been incurred in the production of this volume. The editor is keenly aware of them. I am very grateful to Pj Buchanan for reading, rereading, correcting and editing large sections of the Introduction and Conclusion (and for putting up with me). I am also very grateful to Jenny Pearce for her comments on the early stages of this book. A special debt of gratitude is owed to the editors of *Community Safety Journal*, John Pitts and Chris Fox, and to Pavilion Publishing for allowing us to develop work published in their journal. I would also like to thank my committed, busy and prominent colleagues for taking the time to develop their earlier endeavours into chapters for this book and, most of all, for responding with such good cheer to the changes in editorial arrangements, editorial comments and ridiculously short deadlines that I imposed at various stages throughout the production of this book.

Notes on contributors

Rosie Campbell has carried out applied research on sex work in the UK for over 13 years. She is Chair of the UK Network of Sex Work Projects. She has published widely on sex work. Recent publications include: T. Sanders and R. Campbell (2007) 'Designing out vulnerability, building in respect: violence, safety and sex work policy', *British Journal of Sociology*, vol 58, no 1, pp 1–18; T. Sanders and R. Campbell (2008) 'Why hate men who pay for sex? Exploring the shift to "tackling demand" in the UK', in V.E. Munro and M. della Guista (eds) *Demanding sex: Critical reflections on the regulation of prostitution* (Aldershot: Ashgate); and R. Campbell and M. O'Neill (eds) (2006) *Sex work now* (Cullompton: Willan Publishing).

Justin Gaffney is a nurse with over 15 years' worth of experience establishing and managing frontline sexual health services working with men in the sex industry. In 2007, Justin established SohoBoyz, a new social enterprise in health and social care which focuses on supporting men working in the sex industry from a non-judgemental, harm-minimisation perspective, through training, advocacy and service delivery, creating opportunities for individuals to develop entrepreneurial skills and the capacity to broaden their horizons beyond selling sex.

Phil Hubbard is an urban social geographer who has written widely on issues of sexuality and identity in the city. He is author or co-editor of some nine books, including *Sex and the city: Geographies of prostitution in the urban West* (1999, Aldershot: Ashgate), and is Co-Director of the Centre for Identity, Community and Society at Loughborough University.

Margaret Melrose is Reader in Applied Social Science in the Department of Applied Social Studies, University of Bedfordshire. She has researched the issues of sex work and drug use, particularly among young people, for the past 10 years and has published widely in these fields. Her work has been funded by national bodies such as the Joseph Rowntree Foundation and government departments such as the Home Office and the Department of Health, and has been presented in national and international forums.

Ruth Morgan Thomas has been involved in the sex industry for 29 years: 8 years as a sex worker; 2½ years as an academic researcher at Edinburgh University looking at HIV-related risks in the sex industry; and 18 years as a sex workers' rights advocate developing and seeking to maintain services and support for sex workers within a human rights framework both in the UK and abroad. Ruth is one of the 11 founding members of the Scottish Prostitutes' Education Project (SCOT-PEP) set up in 1989 by sex workers for sex workers in Edinburgh. In 2004 she joined with other sex workers and allies to organise the European Conference on Sex Work, Human Rights, Labour and Migration and is currently Chair of the International Committee for the Rights of Sex Workers in Europe (ICRSE).

Maggie O'Neill is Reader in Criminology and Social Policy at Loughborough University. Her interdisciplinary research career has progressed along a threefold path: the development of cultural, critical and feminist theory; the development of renewed methodologies for sociocultural research – including visual methodologies, ethno-mimesis, and creative consultation; and the development of praxis through participatory action research (PAR) as an outcome of scholarly activity. Together, these contribute to the field of cultural criminology and social policy. Her most recent publications include: *Living and working in areas of street sex work: From conflict to coexistence* (2006, with J. Pitcher, R. Campbell, P. Hubbard, P. Scoular and J. Scoular, Bristol: The Policy Press); *Sex work now* (2006, edited with R. Campbell, Cullompton: Willan Publishing); 'Transnational refugees and the transformative role of art?' (2008, in 'Performative Social Science', a special issue of *Forum for Qualitative Social Research*); and 'Living with the Other: street sex work and contingent communities' (2008, with R. Campbell, P. Hubbard, J. Pitcher and J. Scoular, in *Crime, Media and Culture*, vol 4, no 1).

Jenny Pearce is Professor of Young People and Public Policy at the University of Bedfordshire. Her research interests are young people, sexual exploitation, child protection and domestic violence. Her work explores questions of risk and resilience, gender and sexual identity, domestic and interpersonal violence and adolescence, agency and self-determination. She is on the Board of the UK Network of Sex Work Projects; Chair of the National Working Group on Young People and Sexual Exploitation; and works with local and national government initiatives advancing the rights and interests of sexually exploited young people. Her most recent publications include: *Young people and* *sexual exploitation: Hard to reach and hard to hear* (forthcoming, London: Routledge Falmer); *Growing up with risk* (2007, edited with B. Thom and R. Sales, Bristol: The Policy Press); 'Sex, risk and resilience in adolescence' (2007, in J. Coleman and A. Hagell (eds) *Adolescence, risk and resilience: Against the odds*, Chichester: John Wiley); and 'Finding the "I" in sexual exploitation: hearing the voices of sexually exploited young people in policy and practice' (2006, in R. Campbell and M. O'Neill (eds) *Sex work now*, Cullompton: Willan Publishing).

Jo Phoenix is Reader in Criminology in the School of Applied Social Sciences at Durham University. Her research interests include prostitution, the regulation of sex and youth justice. Her main publications include (with S. Oerton) *Illicit and illegal: Sex, regulation and social control* (2005, Cullompton: Willan Publishing) and *Making sense of prostitution* (2001, London: Palgrave).

Jane Pitcher is an independent social researcher. She has considerable research experience in criminal justice, community safety and social policy and has undertaken a number of studies relating to sex work and services for sex workers. She is the author (with R. Campbell, P. Hubbard, M. O'Neill and J. Scoular) of *Living and working in areas of street sex work: From conflict to coexistence* (2006, Bristol: The Policy Press.)

Teela Sanders is a Senior Lecturer at the University of Leeds. Her research interests are in the relationship between gender, informal economies and regimes of control and she works very much at the intersections of sociology and criminology. She is the author of *Sex work: A risky business* (2005, Cullompton: Willan Publishing); and *Paying for pleasure: Men who buy sex* (2008b, Cullompton: Willan Publishing). In addition, with Harriet Churchill she has written *Getting your PhD* (2007, London: Sage); and with Maggie O'Neill and Jane Pitcher, *Prostitution: Sex work, policy and politics* (2009, London: Sage). Teela has been the Chair of the outreach charity Genesis in Leeds since 2005.

Jane Scoular is Reader in Law at the University of Strathclyde. She has completed numerous theoretical and empirical studies in the area of gender and law. Her work on prostitution brings theoretical insights from feminist and social theory to bear on the issue of sex work and its legal regulation. Recent publications include: J. Scoular and M. O'Neill (2007) 'Regulating prostitution: social inclusion, responsibilisation and the politics of prostitution reform', *British Journal of Criminology*, vol 47, no 5, pp 764–78; P.J. Hubbard, R. Matthews and J. Scoular (2008)

'Re-regulating sex work in the EU: prostitute women and the new spaces of exception', *Gender, Place, Culture*, vol 15, no 2, pp 137–52; and J. Scoular (2009) *The subject of prostitution* (London: Cavendish, Glasshouse Press).

Mary Whowell is a PhD student at Loughborough University working on the geographies of sex work. Her research looks at the ways in which street- and bar-based male sex workers in Manchester practise their sex work, and how their modes of working are affected by different regulatory actors, such as outreach agencies, the police and the city council. It is hoped that the project will allow for some local policy recommendations to be made around sensitive regulation, harm minimisation and safer working. Until moving away from the city, Mary spent a number of years working in a voluntary capacity as an outreach support worker with street- and parlour-based female sex workers, and also with street- and bar-based male sex workers. She is an associate member of the UK Network of Sex Work Projects and is a member of the male sex work working group.

ONE

Frameworks of understanding

Jo Phoenix

Since the turn of the millennium, there has been a proliferation of research and writing on prostitution and the sex industry. Much of it begins with claims about the relative invisibility of the subject – despite the fact that there has been a long and established research tradition within the social sciences in the UK that dates back at least two centuries. The period from the late 1990s to now has witnessed an increased interest in the issue from a wide range of academic disciplines (gender studies, sociology, criminology, psychology, socio-legal studies, urban geography, health studies, pharmacology to name but a few) and practitioners and interest groups (from trade unions representing sex workers to NGOs delivering services, from journalists and other media pundits to campaigning organisations attempting variously to eradicate prostitution or fight for the rights of sex workers, from community organisations to Westminster politicians). Much of that interest is concerned with the question of 'what should be done about prostitution'. While academic debate or discussion has gone on much as it has since the late 1970s, there is something different from before in the tone, tenor and content of public and political discussion. It would seem that, unlike in previous generations, the exchange of sex for money in the UK in the 21st century presents a new type of problem that requires new interventions, new policies and a new approach. Such a renewed interest may well have been further stimulated by the very tragic murders of five women in Ipswich who were all involved in street-based sex work and whose bodies were all found within a few weeks of each other in December 2006.

This book is not about the lives of the men, women and young people who sell sex; nor is this book about their clients, exploiters, abusers, managers, neighbours or other individuals that they come into contact with – although understanding the complexities of the lives of sex workers and others is an important component to the book. This book is about New Labour's attempts to 'do something about' prostitution and the policies and guidance issued by the Home Office and associated other governmental departments and organisations in the early days of the 21st century. The main aim of the book is to give a detailed analysis of the processes, assumptions and contradictions shaping the UK's emerging prostitution policy agenda. Along the way, it describes the impact of the reforms on specific populations of individuals (such as indoor sex workers, street-based sex workers, young people, men or those with drug misuse issues). This book explores the process by which policies are being reformed and the paradoxical conceptual and political agendas that shape them. One of the central objects of inquiry is the way in which the specificity of the contradictions shapes provisions, services and interventions for those in prostitution – arguably a group of people whose social and personal circumstances confound easy categorisation and whose only 'real' commonality is that they sell sex for money. This book addresses a number of fundamental questions: what are the unintended consequences of the recent reforms to prostitution policy? How will the contradictory assumptions shaping the policies impact on the populations that the policies seek to regulate? What are the possibilities, if any, of radical interventions and/or new ways of governing and regulating prostitution that the policies may contain/create? How do the reforms tackle some of the better- and less well-known problems associated with prostitution and the sex industry? What can be learned from other jurisdictions, if anything? What evidence has been used to justify policy change and from where do the policy agendas originate? As a whole, the book makes the claim that unless and until the policy process takes full account of the complex lives of those involved in the commercial exchange of sex for money and the communities in which it takes place, then changes in policy will continue to have paradoxical, ironic and adverse effects on the very people it is trying to help.

This introductory chapter opens with a description of the empirical realities that shape and have shaped many women's choice to sell sex – realities that have remained constant for some time now. From there the chapter provides the reader with two frameworks for understanding: the first, for understanding the shifting discourses which currently constitute prostitution, the second for understanding prostitution policies. Following on from these frameworks, the chapter provides the reader with a narrative framework in which recent policy changes can be placed.

Those readers who are already familiar with the research and literature on prostitution will no doubt find this introduction a rather simplistic overview of the field; but for those who are unfamiliar, the following words of caution may be helpful. There is very little consensus between academics, policy makers or campaigners about either what prostitution 'is' or how best to understand it. Indeed, one of the constitutive elements in the discourses of prostitution has been the ascription of an almost endless variety of social or personal characteristics to those who sell sex. I have written elsewhere that there are four dominant themes by which individuals in prostitution are made sense of (Phoenix, 2001). While earlier research has focused, *inter alia*, on examining the supposedly moral, biological, psychological or sociological pathologies, deficiencies or dysfunctions that are assumed to be the 'causes' of prostitution, contemporary research starts with the assumption that sex work is not separate or distinct from other social, ideological, political and economic structures within society. But there the consensus ends – or at least, the consensus between academics and campaigners. As will be demonstrated in the following chapters, there is an increasing division between academic work on prostitution, which recognises the complexity of sex workers' lives, and political campaigning work, which by definition seeks to flatten that complexity in order to intervene. Notwithstanding this, the description below necessarily abridges much of what we know, in order to focus on the relatively uncontroversial and well-established empirical realities that structure the lives of those individuals who are involved in prostitution.

Selling sex: empirical realities

Two centuries of research on the empirical realities of selling sex in the UK has told a remarkably consistent tale. For the most part, it is women who sell sex and men who buy it. Now, just as when Mayhew (1861) did his survey of Victorian London, selling sex is a form of economic survivalism in an environment where many women have few opportunities for independent financial and social security. Despite the vast social changes that have taken place in the last two centuries, empirical research continues to highlight women's inequality relative to men. So, the European Commission's *Report on equality between men and women* (2008) demonstrates that, regardless of the upheavals in traditional social structures, women's economic and social stability remains mediated by and through their relationships with men and with their families. Throughout Europe, women's pay is on average 15% lower than men's and while there have been increases in the overall numbers of women coming into employment, there have also been dramatic decreases in employment rates for women with children (European Commission, 2008). For those who are in employment, the labour market they enter remains highly segregated, both in terms of occupational hierarchy and in terms of the employment sector

(European Commission, 2008). Seventy-five per cent of part-time workers are women, compared to less than 10% of men; in addition, temporary contracts and long-term unemployment are more common for women than for men (European Commission, 2008). Linked to these employment and pay patterns is women's much higher risk of poverty and the attendant social and personal difficulties that accompany it in the form of homelessness and housing difficulties, poor health and so on (European Commission, 2008). Empirical data also indicate that particular groups of women face substantially higher risks of poverty, including the young, the old, lone parents, the disabled and those who have experienced domestic violence and/or sexual abuse (European Commission, 2006). In the UK, 12 years of New Labour's poverty reduction strategies and welfare benefit reforms have not improved the situation markedly. Instead, these reforms have focused on the 'low-hanging fruit' (that is, those just below the poverty line whose situation can be ameliorated relatively easily) and on 'lifting' children out of poverty. The key strategy has been to get women into work, instead of providing them with financial and economic security through welfare benefits. This has meant that many young women, women without children and women outside the labour market remain in poverty (Bellamy et al, 2006). In the face of this kind of empirical evidence, the notion that women's lives in late modernity are marked by much greater freedoms than ever seen before seems more rhetorical than actual – at least for the significant minority of largely poor, working-class women who still face broadly similar conditions of existence as those faced in previous generations.

The same social and economic structures and processes that maintain women's economic dependency on, and shape their poverty relative to, men also condition their entrance into prostitution (McLeod, 1982; Phoenix, 2001). In this context, sex remains – as ever – a marketable commodity in women's attempts to provide for themselves without recourse to dependency on the state or individual men. In addition to the question of poverty and economic necessity, research into prostitution has also recounted that the backgrounds of many (but by no means all) individuals in prostitution are marked by childhoods spent in local authority care, by physical, sexual and emotional abuse within families and by partners, drug and alcohol problems, running away, housing problems, mental health difficulties and so on. This is especially the case for street-based sex workers. Against this backdrop of poverty and of lives marked by abuse and personal difficulties, prostitution comes to make sense in that it is seen as a strategy by which an individual can escape poverty, dependency on state welfare benefits or on men or their families. As I wrote in an earlier study of street-based sex workers:

> The social, material and ideological conditions that circumscribed the interviewees' earlier lives by structuring their poverty, their community and social ostracism and their dependence on men or state welfare benefits led them to see prostitution as a way forward and a realistic (and successful) strategy for achieving independence, financial and housing security and new social networks. But there was a paradox in the interviewees' narratives. For at the same time as describing it as a means to achieve economic and social stability, they also described it as a 'trap' that further circumscribed their lives and brought even greater poverty, social ostracism, exploitation, abuse, housing difficulties, dependence on men, and thus threatened their social, material and at times physical survival. (Phoenix, 2001: 100)

In short, prostitution often can also be a form of gendered victimisation. Selling sex places those who do so at greater risk of violence, of exploitation, of poverty and of criminalisation (Phoenix, 2001). Rape, kidnapping, brutality, exploitation and other forms of violence have long since been part of the landscape of prostitution – with street-working women experiencing some of the most extreme instances. Like women's entrance into prostitution, such risks are structured by wider gendered relationships, especially the widespread social acceptance of male violence against women and ideologies of femininity that construct sex workers as bad women, as disposable women and women beyond the pale. In this way, it is possible to characterise involvement in prostitution as both a form of gendered survivalism and a form of gendered victimisation (see Phoenix, 2001).

As Matthews (2008) has noted, there is indeed a considerable degree of agreement about sex workers' conditions of existence. The empirical realities have long since been established. What sense is made of those realities, however, becomes a point of contestation. For some, evidence of abuse, exploitation, the role of drugs and the host of other personal and social welfare problems that often (but not always) accompany prostitution – especially from the streets – is emphasised and located as a causal dynamic in an overarching explanation of prostitution as violence against women (see O'Neill and Morgan Thomas in this volume). For others, the economic dynamic is highlighted in a wider explanation of sex work as work (see Morgan Thomas in this volume). For many others, there is no point trying to isolate one or another variable in an attempt to address the question of causation or provide a once-and-for-all characterisation of what prostitution *is* in contemporary British society. For them, it is sufficient to note that selling sex is an economic exchange (no matter what the conditions that surround that exchange) and, as such, the bottom line in sex work will always be money. For the authors in this collection, it is not sufficient to collapse the complex lives that have been and are led by individual sex workers into their personal economic motivations. Instead, it is important to contextualise the choices that individuals make (including the choice to exchange sex for money) when faced with broader social, economic, political and ideological conditions that they have not chosen.

Prostitution and its associations: trafficking, drugs, abuse and consent

Even though the realities of women's lives in prostitution may not have changed in the last two centuries, the discourses shaping how we make sense of them have, particularly since the late 1980s. It is worthy of note that many of these changes have occurred in conjunction with the official 'recognition' of the actual experiences individuals have when they sell sex (that is, poverty, abuse, violence, marginalisation, stigma and so on) (see Phoenix and Oerton, 2005). But, as argued in the Conclusion of this book, in the policy reform process only particular realities of prostitution have been highlighted. In so doing, an ideological landscape has been created that is populated by, first, several categorical and metonymic[1] associations, and second, the emergence and re-emergence of several constitutive binary distinctions. At a conceptual level, these changes both flatten the diversity of experiences of selling sex and serve to blur important boundaries, and ultimately create the conditions for policy reforms that are not capable of dealing with the complexity and distinctiveness of prostitution, as the authors in this book argue.

I use the term 'categorical and metonymic association' to describe the discursive process by which 'prostitution' becomes categorically associated with other social phenomena in ways that make it possible for those other phenomena to act as a proxy. It is *categorical* because the process involves assigning the exchange of sex to a *category* of social problems in relation both to seriousness and type. It is *metonymic* because the two social phenomena become associated in a way that means that one can stand for the other. Take, for instance, the recent identification of the links between global migration and prostitution. Recognition of the mass movement of people (usually women) from around the globe into the sex industry in more affluent Western societies has conditioned the almost complete collapse of any discursive boundary between human trafficking and prostitution. In responding to the international call to do something about human trafficking and the misery, exploitation and human tragedies which trafficking often involves, and in an endeavour to stop illegal migration, governments around the world have focused their attention on prostitution. In an article analysing the passage of the Trafficking Victims' Protection Act 2000 in the USA, Chapkis (2003) argues that strategic use was made of social anxieties around sex, sexual abuse, victimisation and gender in order to usher in greater migration controls in the USA. Fundamental to this was a process by which '*severe forms of trafficking*' became a metonym for *prostitution*, which in the American context is illegal (Chapkis, 2003). The importance is that state responses then turn on an assessment of whether the woman concerned knew that she would end up selling sex: if she did, then she is treated as an illegal migrant; if she did not, she is treated as a victim of trafficking. Similarly, Kempadoo (2005) demonstrates that, as far as the development of international law is concerned, governments have increasingly treated the issue of human trafficking as though the 'problem' of human trafficking is a 'problem' of human trafficking *into sex work*. As the various contributions to Kempadoo's (2005) book make clear, this has resulted in adverse consequences on the anti-trafficking movement, on individual victims of trafficking and on sex workers around the globe. In a similar vein, O'Connell Davidson (2006) explored the ways in which discussions on human trafficking in the UK are also shaped by a conflation of the meanings of human trafficking with prostitution. Central to O'Connell Davidson's article is the recognition that the foundational claims (that human trafficking is happening on a massive scale around the globe, that trafficked persons are modern-day slaves and that most persons trafficked in the UK are trafficked into prostitution) are based more upon a particular rhetorical turn than on detailed empirical evidence. She wrote:

> Meanwhile, feminist abolitionist groups such as Coalition Against Trafficking in Women (CATW) view trafficking as central to, and emblematic of, the increasing globalisation of female sexual exploitation ... Feminist abolitionists hold that it is impossible for women to consent to prostitute, since prostitution dehumanises and objectifies women.

> Prostitution is therefore a form of slavery, and since nobody
> can elect to be a slave, all prostitutes have been trafficked
> into their condition. (O'Connell Davidson, 2006: 8)

Leaving aside the metonymy that marks feminist abolitionist campaigns, there has been widespread belief that more and more women in the sex trade in the UK are there through trafficking – even though there is little empirical evidence to attest to this. As Matthews (2008) pointed out, police forces outside London have a very limited knowledge of the issue of trafficking. A much-quoted Home Office report claimed that between 142 and 1,420 women and children were trafficked into prostitution in the UK (Kelly and Regan, 2000). These numbers were derived by a methodological sleight of hand in which the authors collected figures from 36 police constabularies about *actual* known trafficking cases (which for 1998 numbered 71) and combined these with: figures from the police about ongoing cases; figures from the Immigration Service about suspected cases in which women were trafficked *through* the UK and the origins of women entering the UK as overseas wives; police figures about the numbers of foreign nationals working in the Soho area of London; reports from health project workers about the suspected percentage of women who might have been trafficked; newspaper reports about the presence of supposedly trafficked women in areas of the UK; and a survey of internet sites advertising off-street sex work venues. Using these figures, Kelly and Regan (2000) speculated that the 'real' number of women trafficked into prostitution was somewhere between two and 20 times more than that which had been confirmed, and thus claimed that between 142 and 1,420 women per year were trafficked for prostitution in the UK. Despite what is said, these figures do not represent guestimates of the numbers of women being trafficked in the UK for prostitution. Instead, they are a set of figures calculated on the basis that at least a proportion of women in the above categories *may be* trafficked into prostitution. In all fairness to the authors of the report, they recognise that it is not possible to know with any degree of certainty the 'true' extent of women being trafficked. Notwithstanding that authorial qualification, the starting point for their methodological assumption, which perhaps is something that should be challenged, was that, as it could not be known that the women in the various categories above were *not* trafficked, it should therefore be assumed that some had been. To extend the logic of this methodological assumption: perhaps Kelly and Regan should have also included a percentage extracted from the total number of all women using any public transport in London, for, in common with the category they did use, we cannot know with certainty that some of the women using London transport are not being trafficked!

The figure of between 142 and 1,420 perhaps tells the informed reader that, despite political and rhetorical claims about trafficking and prostitution, the inability to quantify the issue more precisely is indicative of how *little* is *actually* known. More recently, and following Operation Pentameter in 2006 (described by the press as a 'crackdown on human smuggling'), the Metropolitan Police claimed that up to 18,000 women and children were trafficked into prostitution in the UK. Yet, only 84 individuals were actually identified as victims of trafficking. It is worth quoting at length a letter written by O'Connell Davidson and published in the *Guardian*, to show just how much hyperbole is used when reporting or quoting statistics on trafficking:

> Harriet Harman holds that a Swedish-style law against buying sex is necessary to stem demand for sex workers trafficked into Britain (Harman calls for prostitution ban, December 21). She was supported by former Europe minister Denis MacShane, who insisted there are 25,000 sex slaves in the UK. This is a startling assertion – 25,000 is more than the entire workforce of Debenhams. How is it that this vast number of women and girls are so readily available to male clients and yet simultaneously so difficult for the police to detect? When 515 indoor prostitution establishments were raided by police as part of Operation Pentameter last year, only 84 women and girls who conformed to police and immigration officers' understanding of the term 'victim of trafficking' were 'rescued'. At this rate, the police would need to raid some 150,000 indoor prostitution establishments to unearth MacShane's 25,000 sex slaves. The fact that there are estimated to be fewer than 1,000 such establishments in London gives some indication of how preposterous MacShane's claim is. (Prof Julia O'Connell Davidson, *Guardian*, 28 December 2007)

The power of these exaggerated claims about the growing problem of trafficking and prostitution has been felt in relation to policy. The 2003 Sexual Offences Act makes it an offence to knowingly transport women for the purposes of sexual exploitation – a provision that is worryingly unclear on whether a taxi driver transporting a woman who s/he knows to be a sex worker could now be prosecuted under provisions geared towards disrupting human trafficking. The UK Action Plan on Tackling Human Trafficking followed the establishment of the UK Human Trafficking Centre and a host of other specific Home Office-funded initiatives, such as the Poppy Project. Most of the guidelines, proscriptions and changes to law have been focused on trafficking *for the purposes of sexual exploitation,* even though in consultation documents and final reports some attention is paid to forced labour and illegal migration. In this policy context, sexual exploitation serves as a metonymy for prostitution, with the result that human trafficking and prostitution become treated as though they are proxies for one another.

Government and policy discussion is framed by the almost complete negation of trafficking as existing as anything other than prostitution. The difficulty inherent in such a categorical metonymic association is that the social, historical and political specificity of the migration and movement of women, men and children into and within the UK *and* the specificity of prostitution are obscured. So, for instance, the young person transported across Europe, or across the globe, to work in a distant relative's legitimate business gets lost. Similarly, the specificities of women's experiences of poverty and of migration that are not connected to work in the sex industry also get lost. In policy terms, this means that policies addressing prostitution become a means to address the exploitative and illegal migration of people, just as policies addressing *trafficking* become a means to address the commercial exchange of sex for money. The problem becomes one and the same thing. For example, in March 2007 the BBC reported that 'Sex slavery [is] widespread in England'. Two statements in this report stand out as important. First, the UK Human Trafficking Centre reported cases in which impoverished English women were being sold and transported from town to town in the UK to work as prostitutes. Second, in the mid 1990s it was estimated that 85% of the women who worked in brothels in London were English, whereas by 2007 it was estimated that 85% of the women in London brothels were from overseas. With that, 'the problem' of prostitution becomes a problem of migration, and the migration of women becomes a problem of prostitution. In general, and perhaps more important still, the tone, tenor and debate surrounding prostitution within the UK takes on a new sense of urgency – and one which is marked by the re-emergence of state-sponsored Salvationism, that is, in which the state is positioned as saviour, rescuing the hapless victims of international criminal activity (see especially O'Connell Davidson, 2005). Of course, the association of prostitution and the forced, coerced or exploitative movement of women does have a long historical legacy in the UK. Moral panics about 'the white slave trade' in the late Victorian period ushered in legislation which both raised the age of consent for girls from 13 to 16 (1885 Sexual Offences Amendment Act) and generated new forms of regulation and control for working-class women more generally (see Walkowitz, 1980).

While I have focused on the categorical and metonymic association of human trafficking and prostitution, there are other such associations that now mark the discourse of prostitution. As Melrose argues in this volume, there is another almost complete collapse between how drugs markets and the problems of drug addiction are conceptualised and how street-based prostitution is conceptualised. At the risk of repetition, at the theoretical level, collapsing the boundaries between prostitution and other social 'problems' (in this case drugs and drug addiction) results in obscuring the specificity and complexity of both prostitution and drug addiction. At the level of policy and practice, it results in the adoption of interventions and policies designed to deal with one social problem being seen by government as appropriate to deal with another. A further categorical and metonymic association that has occurred in the UK has been the association of prostitution with community safety concerns, as Scoular et al explore in this volume. So, even though the empirical realities of selling sex may not have changed in the last few centuries, how prostitution is conceived, conceptualised and understood has. The categorical and metonymic association between prostitution and human trafficking, migration and smuggling, prostitution and sexual exploitation, prostitution and drugs, and prostitution and incivility or anti-sociality has created the conditions in which, in terms of policy, prostitution rarely gets treated as the commercial exchange of sex for money and instead is treated as though it were something else (as all the contributors to this volume attest).

Earlier I mentioned that the contemporary discourses of prostitution are also shaped by the emergence and re-emergence of several important binary distinctions: these centre on the question of consent. Recognition of the very real and present risks of violence and exploitation faced by many sex workers has served to ignite debate about whether those involved in prostitution are forced or coerced into it or whether their involvement is chosen or voluntary. Such binary distinctions function in such a way that the question of economic necessity has been largely displaced in an endeavour to show that individuals selling sex are sex slaves, economic entrepreneurs or offenders and threats to community safety, stability and security. With that, older constructions of sex workers either as deserving victims in need of rescue or as undeserving, immoral, disreputable and/or criminal have re-emerged and, as Scoular et al and

O'Neill in this volume demonstrate, have found particular expression in the recent reforms to policy. The question of consent takes on significant meaning in contemporary debates, particularly in relation to the issue of age. At the theoretical and policy level, distinctions drawn between adults in prostitution and commercially sexually exploited children have had profound effects. Policies have been created on the assumption that any person under the age of 18 years cannot consent to commercial sex exchanges, and thus any exchange that occurs is by definition an act of sexual abuse (or, in contemporary parlance, sexual exploitation). Notwithstanding the fact that the age of sexual consent in the UK is 16 years, such a binary distinction (child victim, adult sex worker) belies the very complex realities experienced by many young people and adults, and blurs the boundaries between sexual exploitation and child sexual abuse. Paradoxically, this age distinction also underpins the 'persistent returners' clause in policy by which young people who are assessed as *voluntarily* and persistently returning to prostitution are seen as appropriate subjects for criminal justice intervention rather than for child protection and statutory welfare service provision (see also Phoenix, 2002, 2004). As Pearce notes later in the volume, it also serves to locate provision for sexually exploited young people firmly within child protection statutory services.

In short, the discourse of prostitution and the ideological conditions which shape that discourse have changed markedly since the late 1970s – even though the poverty, criminalisation, violence, abuse and stigma that so many of the UK's sex workers experience have not. In contemporary Britain, 'prostitution' is becoming a very dense signifier around which a variety of social anxieties (about age, abuse, consent, the relationship between money and sex, drugs, the movement of women and children within the country and around the globe, disease and so on) find expression. This is a theme that I will return to in the Conclusion to this volume. Suffice it to say here that the way in which prostitution has become equated with a number of easily sensationalised phenomena (such as child abuse and human trafficking, drugs and crime and so on) may well have contributed to the final key change that has occurred in the last few years – its place on the political landscape. As an issue, it has moved up the social and political agenda, as evidenced by the wealth of media reporting, television documentaries, academic and scholarly research and, of course, policy reform. The next section begins to untangle some of the confusion that surrounds prostitution policy and its objectives, and the different models of intervention that exist.

Objectives of policy? Regulating prostitution

One of the abiding dynamics in regulating prostitution has been the tendency of those who make policy to specify the distinct social or individual characteristics of those involved in selling sex – characteristics that both explain their involvement in prostitution and mark them as different from the rest of the population. This process of creating binary distinctions between sex workers and others (that is, 'normal' women, children and so on) is not new. For instance, British legislators in the mid-19th century departed from the then contemporary understanding of prostitution as being a matter of sin and morality by defining it instead as a threat to the health of the nation. The 1864, 1866 and 1869 Contagious Diseases Acts created a legislative framework that forced medical examinations and treatment on women suspected of being prostitutes. The result was the symbolic and literal segregation of women in prostitution. Similarly, the Wolfenden Committee's Report on Prostitution and Homosexual Offences (Wolfenden Committee Report, 1957) defined prostitution as a matter of private morality except where the presence of 'immoral' women caused affront to decent citizens and provided the basis for a set of laws which focused almost exclusively on regulating the visibility of sex work and sex workers. As I argued above, one of the important changes in the last few decades has been the emergence of a set of particular binary distinctions that operate both to blur the edges of prostitution into other social phenomena (such as child sexual abuse, trafficking, drug abuse, a lack of community safety, violence against women, anti-social behaviour and so on) and to compress the diversity and complexity of the social experiences of sex workers. Such changes in how sex workers are perceived are important to note, as any understanding of what 'the problem' of prostitution is contains within it the suggestion of a model or type of intervention.

It is possible to discern four main objectives to how commercial sexual exchanges are dealt with by government. To put it another way, when governments do choose to intervene and create laws or policies on prostitution, they do so for a wider purpose or aim. First, governments can use a combination of formal legislation and social policies in order to eliminate the exchange of sex for money (known commonly as *abolitionism* and/or *prohibitionism*). Abolitionism and prohibitionism are often distinguished on political grounds. Abolitionism is usually situated within feminist discourse and constructs prostitution as violence against women.[2] Despite the declared aim of eliminating prostitution, abolitionists will often also aim to protect sex workers from further criminalisation. By contrast, prohibitionism is more often situated within discourses that constitute sex work as immoral. Second, governments may intervene in prostitution with the purpose of reducing the dangers and harms of working in prostitution (known as *harm minimisation* or *reductionism*). Harm minimisation or reductionism is located within public health discourse, wherein the key objective is to reduce or prevent the problems associated with prostitution. It originated during the 1980s as a means of dealing with problematic drug use. Fundamental to harm minimisation is the development of a non-judgemental approach to sex workers. So, for Plant (1997), harm minimisation is 'value neutral' towards the behaviour that is addressed (whether that is drug and alcohol misuse or prostitution). Third, governments may intervene with the aim of increasing the employment and human rights of sex workers (known as a *rights-based* approach). A rights-based approach to prostitution is located within juridico-legal discourse and identifies 'the problem' of prostitution as being the lack of legal rights (and the lack of enforcement of human rights) of sex workers (Edwards, 1997). Fourth, the aim or objective of policy may be only to manage or control what are perceived as the more disruptive activities, relationships or elements of the trade (also known as *regulationism* and/or *regulated tolerance*). Regulationism (or indeed regulated intolerance, negative regulationism and so on) is an approach that is not located within any particular discourse of prostitution, but rather a discourse of pragmatism in which sex work is accepted as a 'social fact' and efforts are made simply to manage what is seen as being a problematic, informal industry (Matthews, 1986; 2008).

Models of intervention

These objectives, or broader aims of policy, should not be confused with models of intervention, which are the strategies and techniques by which governments can implement their aims or objectives. More, there is no necessary connection between any particular objective of policy and/or the various models of intervention. That said, abolitionism or prohibitionism, and regulationism, tend to make strategic use of criminal justice interventions and primary legalisation in achieving those aims. By contrast, soft policy, government guidance and the strategic use of funding to non-governmental welfare organisations working with those involved in sex work are often the means by which the aim of harm reductionism or minimisation is usually achieved. The aim of increasing the rights of sex workers is usually implemented through the legalisation of prostitution, or the legalisation of a limited range of prostitution-related activities. In this way many countries may share the same basic framework of legislation, but the actual aim of policies can be fundamentally dissimilar. There are very few jurisdictions that have a singular objective. In practice, the objectives of policy are usually multiple and often contradictory. Similarly, the different models of intervention – criminalisation, decriminalisation and legalisation – seldom find singular expression in practice. When analysing law and policy, most jurisdictions have a mixed model, and for that reason each model of intervention finds quite distinct expressions in practice. The following discussion provides a description of each model as it exists in the abstract, with some exemplars from different jurisdictions and a very brief discussion of some of the known difficulties or unintended consequences.

Criminalisation

The criminalisation of prostitution is a model of intervention in which the criminal law is used to manage, control, repress, prohibit or otherwise influence the growth, instance or expression of prostitution. Within such a model, prostitution is defined primarily as a criminal justice issue, as opposed to a moral, health or human rights issue. The problems of prostitution are seen as being similar to those caused by other criminal behaviours. Typically, particular types of prostitution-related activities are defined as causing the kind of harm that warrants the use of criminal justice sanction and punishment. In reality there are few jurisdictions that have implemented a model of intervention that fully criminalises all aspects of prostitution; exceptions are large parts of the USA, the Middle East and some parts of Europe, such as Romania, where the selling of sex and all associated activities are illegal. In Romania, prostitution can attract a prison sentence of up to 7 years. By contrast, most other jurisdictions only deploy criminal justice sanctions to manage, contain, repress or prohibit specified prostitution-related activities. Disregarding the notable exceptions listed above, it is more appropriate to speak of partial criminalisation, as this is more usual. Thus, in the UK, criminal justice sanctions are brought to bear on the public nuisance associated with prostitution (that is, the *visibility* of sex workers), through making it illegal to solicit or loiter in a public place for the purposes of prostitution; and on the ability of third parties to make pecuniary gains from those involved in selling sex, through criminalising the commercial exploitation of children or adults in prostitution. One of the unintended consequences of such partial criminalisation has been the relative over-policing of women's prostituting activities and the under-policing of the crimes committed against them. Take, for example, the provision in the 1956 Sexual Offences Act against 'living off the earnings of prostitution', that is, pimping and 'exercising control over a prostitute', that is, brothel keeping. In 2003, 30 convictions and four cautions were secured for living off earnings of prostitution or exercising control over a prostitute. The same year saw 2,627 convictions and 902 cautions for soliciting or loitering in a public place for the purposes of prostitution.[3] The importance of these statistics is not just the demonstration that women in prostitution tend to be over-policed, although this is certainly worthy of note; rather, that the consequence of regulating prostitution through criminalising women's prostituting activities is that the women bear the burden of intervention and, more important, of punishment.

In England and Wales the usual punishment for prostitution-related offences is a fine. The irony herein is that many women, particularly those working from outdoor locations, are precisely those for whom prostitution is a result of poverty. In this fashion, criminal justice responses become part of the dynamic that holds women in prostitution.

Other jurisdictions have defined the criminality of prostitution very differently. In 1999, Swedish feminist campaigns were successful in achieving an official definition of prostitution as being a problem of sexual violence against women and thereby reorienting policies towards abolitionism. As a result, Swedish law now criminalises men *purchasing* sex instead of criminalising women who sell it. While there is some debate about the extent to which the criminalisation of the purchasing of sex has achieved an overall reduction in prostitution, given that Swedish levels of prostitution have been historically low, criminalising the purchasing of sex has produced anomalous results. Many Swedish social workers have reported that some of the women who had been selling sex from the streets have now been forced to move into illegal brothels or to work alone from indoor locations. Such a move leaves these women more isolated than before, which arguably exposes them to greater risks of violence and leaves them open to exploitation at the hands of brothel keepers. Furthermore, there are also reports that it has become substantially more dangerous for those women who continue to sell sex from the streets. Some women report that because there are fewer clients prepared to go to street-working women, many are willing to accept greater sums offered for unprotected sex, or will go with clients before they have had a chance to fully assess them as potentially dangerous (Ericksson, 2005; Jacobsson, 2006; see also Svanström, 2006). In this way, criminalising the purchase of sex in order to provide greater protection for women in prostitution has had the paradoxical effect of generating higher levels of risk and danger. Thus, one of the perverse consequences of intervening in prostitution through the mechanism of criminal justice is that it often increases, rather than decreases, the levels of riskiness, vulnerability and poverty of women in prostitution, especially those women who tend to be targeted most – street-based sex workers.

Legalisation

The legalisation of prostitution is a model of intervention in which some or all criminal justice sanctions regarding the sale and purchase of sex are removed and replaced by civic regulations regarding the legal status of the contract between the seller and the purchaser of sex, and the conditions in which it is permissible to sell sex. The legalisation of prostitution confers important contractual rights to individuals in prostitution and provides a means through which the working conditions of those in the sex industry can be monitored and improved. In this respect, legalised prostitution is fundamentally different from a model of intervention in which the sale of sex is legal, but where the criminal justice system is used as the *primary* means of managing the sex industry generally. For example, since 2001, prostitution in Germany has been legally recognised as a profession. The contract between sex workers and clients can be legally enforced through the civil courts and the conditions in which women work fall under other employment health and safety directives (as well as specific occupation-related health and safety provision). That said, the legal recognition of prostitution in Germany does not mean that prostitution has the same status as other occupations. Employment centres do not advertise jobs in prostitution, women in receipt of state benefits are not penalised if they do not take a job within prostitution; prostitution-related occupations are taxed at a higher rate and local municipalities retain the right to zone areas of the city wherein prostitution is not permitted. In Munich, street prostitution is not permitted throughout most of the city; in Berlin it is allowed almost anywhere; while Hamburg permits street prostitution only in particular areas and at particular times.

Many countries that legalise prostitution can also require sex workers to register with a licensing authority, the local authority or local courts. This may also, occasionally, involve compulsory health checks for sex workers or a range of other proscriptions. So, for instance, in the Netherlands individuals have to be 18 years and older to be sex workers, but only 16 years old to be clients, while in Greece it is not possible for married women to register as prostitutes.

Two of the difficulties of legalising prostitution are providing a mechanism by which individuals can enforce their legal and contractual rights, and ensuring that the interests of business do not dominate the legal trade. Evidence from Germany would indicate that while sex workers are now entitled to the same sort of legal rights conferred to any worker vis-à-vis social security and employment protection, claiming those benefits has proved to be very difficult (Mitrovic, 2004). For instance, labour law is difficult if not impossible to apply to the private relationship between a sex worker and her boyfriend/partner who may be exploiting her prostituting activities. Similarly, because many of the women working in legal brothels are casually employed, enforcing their labour rights is as difficult as is enforcing the labour rights of other workers in predominantly low-paid, casual employment. The legalisation of the sex trade in Germany has done little to stop the illegal sex trade; evidence also suggests that legalisation has done little to ameliorate the stigma of being a sex worker or even, necessarily, to improve the working conditions of women in prostitution (Mitrovic, 2004). It may be that the legalisation of prostitution is a model of intervention that works primarily at a symbolic, rather than a practical level. Thus, in an effort to provide a symbolic message that sex work is work like any other, the implementation of special measures or regulations for sex workers serves to increase the distinction between sex workers and other low-paid, casual and exploited workers – none more so than in systems that require formal registration and compulsory health checks (see also Hubbard, 1999).

Decriminalisation

It is often claimed that the decriminalisation of prostitution amounts to its legalisation. This is not the case. Decriminalisation is the removal of both the battery of criminal justice laws prohibiting prostitution or prostitution-related activities, and any prostitution-related civil regulations discussed above. This does not mean that the sale of sex and prostitution is not subject to law or policy, but rather that it is not subject to special provision, criminal or otherwise. The contract between workers and clients does not constitute a special category of contract and the intervention in sex workers' employment is no different from other industries.

Decriminalisation is framed by the assumption that the stigma of prostitution will cease if it is not treated as though it needs special criminal justice or civil regulations. So, the argument goes, decriminalisation will remove prostitution from discussions of morality or legality. It is argued that decriminalising prostitution would result in sex work taking its place alongside any other profession and that it would be regulated like any other form of employment, that is, by employment legislation and health and safety provisions. Indeed, one of the messages from those campaigning for the decriminalisation of prostitution is that it is the key means of ensuring the safety and health of sex workers and clients, by relocating the instrument of regulation as health and safety in the workplace provisions (Scarlet Alliance, 1999). Very few countries have adopted a wholesale decriminalisation of prostitution, opting instead to decriminalise only brothel prostitution. For instance, in New South Wales, Australia, brothel prostitution is decriminalised but local municipalities still retain the right to pass local ordinances prohibiting street prostitution in specific areas. In contrast, in New Zealand the 2003 Prostitution Reform Act decriminalised all aspects of prostitution, repealing all previous legislation making prostitution and brothel keeping illegal, and confirming that contracts for commercial sexual exchanges could legally exist. That said, New Zealand did not fully decriminalise young people's involvement in prostitution, as criminal justice sanctions can be brought to bear against those who purchase sex from those under the age of 18 years, regardless of the age of sexual consent.

At the time of the reform in New Zealand, many opponents of decriminalisation argued that to remove sanctions or regulations pertaining to prostitution would result in the exponential growth of the sex industry and the infiltration of organised crime into the industry. Interestingly, research reported by New Zealand's Prostitution Law Review Committee on the Operation of the Prostitution Reform Act 2003, in May 2008, claimed not only that there has been no recordable growth in the numbers of individuals involved in prostitution or in trafficking, but that decriminalisation has had a marked effect on safeguarding and protecting the rights and safety of those selling sex (Ministry of Justice, 2008).

The story of reform: the creation of a 'coherent strategy' on prostitution?

In the opening decade of the 21st century, the New Labour government has adopted a clearly abolitionist objective to the regulation of prostitution and is in the process of attempting to create a more 'coherent' model of intervention based on the strategy of criminalisation. The objective of policy reform has been to 'challenge the view that prostitution is inevitable and here to stay [and] achieve an overall reduction in street prostitution' (Home Office, 2006: 1). New Labour is advocating an 'enforcement plus support' strategy in which women are diverted into welfare services in order that they can be encouraged to exit prostitution or else face the full range of criminal justice disposals. Importantly, current proposals are to create compulsory rehabilitation orders for sex workers wherein attendance at a variety of welfare services (such as drugs services, sex workers' projects and the like) will be made compulsory, and sanctionable if breached. The vision of this 'coherent' strategy is that, through compelling women to seek help, more and more women will end up leaving prostitution, and the overall objective can be achieved. The full details of the UK's prostitution policies and the reform process will not be provided in this Introduction, but are described in the chapters that follow.

Until the last decade, inasmuch as a 'prostitution policy' existed in the UK it was little more than a piecemeal amalgam of case law, statute and government guidance to police constabularies, local authorities or other statutory organisations in which various prostitution-related activities were regulated. If anything 'united' this disparate set of policies it was the injunction put forward by the Wolfenden Committee, that the law had no place intervening in prostitution *except* when the activities of prostitutes or their clients caused affront to ordinary citizens or when those in prostitution were exploited. Hence, selling sex is not illegal and criminal justice sanctions focus on visible prostitution, that is, loitering and soliciting in public places. The period from the 1980s to the turn of the millennium did, however, see substantial changes in relation to social, health and welfare provisions for sex workers, and in many ways paved the ground for the establishment of a 'prostitution policy' in the UK. So the 1980s saw a growth in sexual health outreach services designed for sex workers as an attempt to reduce the risks associated with the spread of sexually transmitted infections, and in particular the spread of HIV/AIDS. The growth of these sexual health outreach organisations also saw a shift in policing and a dramatic reduction in the numbers of women being cautioned or arrested for prostitution-related offences (see Phoenix, 2008). By the late 1990s, we begin to see the emergence of a binary distinction between children and adults in prostitution, and with that a series of policy reforms that shaped separate types of intervention depending on the age of the individual involved in commercial sexual exchanges. The Department of Health and the Home Office issued joint guidance to all local authorities and statutory organisations (DH/HO, 2000). As indicated above, the guidance stated that children and young people (that is, those under the age of 18 years) involved in prostitution should not be criminalised in the first instance, but should be treated as victims of child sexual abuse and subsequently dealt with via social services and other children's agencies. So the conceptual distinction led almost directly to policy reform which has had the effect of splitting provision for sex workers into services for children and services for adults, with services for adults remaining orientated to criminalisation and harm minimisation and services for those under the age of 18 years old arising from and orientated towards child protection. In relation to criminal justice, the latter half of the 20th century saw the criminalisation of kerb crawling and the removal of the prison sentences for women convicted of soliciting or loitering for prostitution. By the turn of the millennium, the UK bore witness to a system of intervention that acted in an ad hoc and highly localised manner (see Phoenix, 2008). Since then, however, the situation has changed. It is now possible to argue that the UK has something that might be called a 'prostitution policy', in that the different threads of policy and reforms to policy have been drawn together under one strategy that has a 'new' explicitly stated purpose and approach (as will be shown in the contributions in this volume) and primary legislation has been introduced for two consecutive years in line with that explicitly stated purpose.

It is tempting to say that the creation of *A Coordinated Prostitution Strategy* was the result of policy work on or around prostitution and sex work alone. It would, however, be more accurate to situate the emergence of the UK's prostitution policy in the late 1990s review of sexual offences. As will be demonstrated in the chapters in this book, the rhetoric shaping *A Coordinated Prostitution Strategy* comes almost directly from the rhetoric shaping the review of sexual offences. In January 1999 the then Home Secretary, Jack Straw, commissioned an independent body to review the laws on sexual offences and to make recommendations that would create a legal framework that would be coherent, fair and non-discriminatory in relation to the European Convention on Human Rights and the 1998 Human Rights Act, would protect individuals from sexual abuse and exploitation, and ensure that those found guilty would be properly punished. The findings of the Sexual Offences Review (published as *Setting the Boundaries: Reforming the Law on Sexual Offences, Parts I & II*, Home Office, 2000) formed the basis of a White Paper (*Protecting the Public*, Home Office, 2002) and were mostly adopted in the 2003 Sexual Offences Act.

Arguably, the call to reform sexual offences legislation was shaped in part by New Labour's modernising agenda, or at the very least by a rhetoric of modernisation (see also Phoenix and Oerton, 2005), which was very prevalent in the early days of the first New Labour government. It was also conditioned by the growing awareness that attitudes about sex and sexuality had fundamentally changed between the 1956 Sexual Offences Act, the 1959 Street Offences Act and the end of the 20th century, particularly in regard to the acceptability of homosexuality and the separation of sex and sexuality from the traditional institutions of marriage and the family. But perhaps of much greater significance were the decades of largely feminist research and campaigns in and around the area of sexual violence. Throughout the 1980s and 1990s, academics and campaigning organisations – Rape Crisis, Women's Aid and a growing sexual abuse survivors' movement – offered a critique of the content and operation of the laws regarding sex, sexual violation and sexual abuse. This critique focused on three main issues: the problem of definition; the regularity of sexual violation; and the discriminatory way in which victims of sexual violence were dealt with by the criminal justice system. Feminists argued that the legal definitions of rape and other forms of sexual abuse effectively created a hierarchy of abuse in which the only violations that really mattered were rape and the sexual violation of those under the age of 13 years. More particularly, rape was defined so narrowly, that is, a penis penetrating a vagina, that the law offered very little recourse for women whose experiences of violations were much broader. Finally, the legal definitions of all sexual offences centred on the question of consent – a question that placed the burden of proof upon the victim. Burgeoning research literature on sexual violence showed the gulf that existed between legal definitions and actual lived experiences. Rape and other forms of sexual assault were shown not to be rare events committed by men whose sexuality was an aberration of the normal aggressive male sexual drive, but rather by ordinary men as friends, boyfriends, partners, fathers, brothers and the like. The literature also theorised that sexual violence had little to do with sex and much more to do with power and domination. In this way the exceptionally low rates of conviction and high rates of attrition for rape cases were explained as part of the discriminatory way that victims of sexual abuse were treated by the criminal justice system and the courts. The argument ran that the stereotyping of children as liars and of women as 'asking for it', as saying 'no when they meant yes' and so on served to shape the ways that the police investigated allegations of rape, the decisions of the Crown Prosecution Service and the practices and decisions of the courts and juries.

So, by the time New Labour was elected to office, there was a widespread recognition that sexual practices within society had changed, that there was increasing tolerance towards lesbians and gay men, that the law simply did not reflect the realities of sexual violence and abuse and that discrimination against women and children was extensive in the criminal justice system. Arguably, this informed New Labour's decision to draw the scope of the Sexual Offences Review very widely. The Sexual Offences Review Commission was convened to review 'all sexual offences' including the laws regarding rape, sexual assault, consent, child sexual abuse, abuse of trust, the age of consent, 'cottaging', bestiality, indecent exposure, voyeurism, sexual interference with human remains, as well as the commercial exploitation of children or adults and trafficking in people for commercial exploitation.

Notwithstanding the declared breadth of the review, prostitution-related laws were excluded from the review process. This was despite the similarity of the critique of the then existing sexual offences legislation and the critique of prostitution laws, and despite the campaigning of sex workers' rights organisations and academics. Arguably, as a result of the process of consultation about sexual offences (published as *Setting the Boundaries*), the then Home Secretary, David Blunkett, announced in the White Paper *Protecting the Public* the government's intention to investigate the possibility of piecemeal reform of prostitution-related offences, to 'examine the scope for a review of the issues surrounding prostitution and the exploitation, organized criminality and class A drug abuse associated with it' (Home Office, 2002: 31). Some two years later the consultation document *Paying the Price* (2004) was published. It did not initiate a full review of prostitution-related offences or a review of the law in regard to prostitution; rather, it consulted on very narrow terms – preventing young people's coercion into or exploitation in prostitution, providing exit strategies for those adults involved in prostitution and providing justice against pimps, traffickers and exploiters for families and communities blighted by prostitution.

The result of this consultation process and the responses, like the consultation document itself, was delayed in publication by nearly a year. *A Coordinated Prostitution Strategy and a summary of responses to 'Paying the Price'* was finally released in January 2006. Despite several high-profile media leaks about the possibility of legalising some brothel work and creating zones of tolerance (or not),[4] *A Coordinated Prostitution Strategy*, as was suggested initially in *Protecting the Public*, made no suggestions for reform of the law.

Importantly, however, these consultation documents provided the rhetorical and ideological justification for a push towards a significant extension of police and criminal justice powers of arrest, prosecution and punishment over the activities and relationships that comprise prostitution, as well as over the women in the sex industry. Indeed, while the consultation documents do not recommend primary legislation, they have nevertheless legitimated the abolitionist stance currently taken by at least two high-level Labour ministers: the former Home Secretary, Jacqui Smith, and the Deputy Leader of the Labour Party, Harriet Harman. Both have supported the introduction of primary legislation for two consecutive years. In 2007, the 2007–2008 Criminal Justice and Immigration Bill included measures to introduce what has been called 'the Swedish model' of criminalising the purchasing of sex. But despite much high-level political support from the Home Office and other high-profile Labour MPs and ministers, the clauses were deleted at the second reading stage. The 2009 Policing and Crime Bill represents a second attempt by the Home Office to introduce primary legislation whose objective is abolitionist and whose mode of intervention is criminalisation. So, clauses 13 and 14 would make it illegal to purchase sex from a prostitute 'controlled for gain'. Clause 16 introduces a 'compulsory' rehabilitation order to anyone convicted of soliciting or loitering for the purposes of prostitution (a measure that was thrown out of the earlier Criminal Justice and Immigration Bill). Clause 18 would make it an offence to solicit anyone in a public place for the purposes of prostitution (as opposed to the current situation in which it is an offence to persistently solicit anyone in a public place, that is, kerb crawling). Clause 20 moves to extend the ASBO-like civil closure orders currently used against 'crack houses' to brothels. Clause 25 would see the reclassification of lap-dancing clubs as 'sex encounter venues' and therefore as establishments that require licensing and that can also be the subject of proceeds of crime legislation.

While the success of the prostitution-related clauses in the 2009 Policing and Crime Bill is unknown at the time of writing, what remains clear is that the last decade has seen a significant adjustment of UK social policies on prostitution towards an abolitionist aim. Arguably, the attempts to criminalise the purchase of sex (from women controlled for gain) and so on represent only one small part of the government's strategy for reform. It is also significant the New Labour has created a raft of new central governmental guidance to local authorities, statutory organisations and non-governmental voluntary organisations, as well as criteria for funding organisations working with individuals in prostitution – for these all act on the day-to-day activities of those working with or coming into regular contact with those in the sex industry. In accordance with the new 'coordinated strategy' of government, all of these guidances, documents, funding criteria and so on are underpinned by a clear abolitionist direction. Simply, even though *A Coordinated Prostitution Strategy* did not recommend new legislation, it signalled the intention of central government to shift the direction and goal of policies pertaining to prostitution, so that whatever else they may achieve, the policies should 'challenge the view that prostitution is inevitable and here to stay [and] achieve an overall reduction in street prostitution' (Home Office, 2006: 1). In so doing, its influence and impact should not be underestimated. It provides the ideological justification for a considerable extension of the criminalisation of prostitution-related activities as well as creating a baseline or yardstick by which local-level policy makers and practitioners shape their work and practice.

The following section describes the organisation of the book. Interwoven with that description is more about the specific details of the UK's prostitution policy reforms, the 'coordinated strategy' that has been adopted and the particular recommendations for practice innovation that are suggested by central government.

The organisation of this book

The book is divided into two sections. The first provides a conceptual examination of the reforms, in chapters that provide a theoretical framework by which it is possible to understand the UK's prostitution policy – also referred to throughout this volume as the strategy on prostitution. This section looks at the different and various ways in which what is perceived as the 'problem of prostitution' is conceptualised by the government. Chapters Two and Three examine the contradictions, underpinning assumptions and unintended consequences of the reforms at a local level. The thematic focus of much of these two chapters is 'community safety', as 'community safety' has been used as the key political justification for the recent changes. The second section of the book provides an in-depth examination of how specific issues related to selling and purchasing sex are dealt with. The authors draw on a range of sources – from empirical research data to professional voluntary organisation experience of practice. Each chapter outlines current practice and examines how and in what ways the policy reforms are beginning to impact in terms of both intended and unintended consequences.

In Chapter Two, Scoular et al situate English reform in relation to abolitionism, concerns about community safety, zero tolerance and violence against women strategies, and call into question one of the key assumptions made by New Labour: that prostitution presents problems of anti-social behaviour and is not tolerated within communities. By reflecting on a recent study conducted by the authors, they argue that the empirical data point to some of the dangers of creating a prostitution policy that continues to situate sex work as antithetical to the cultivation of community safety. Offering a critical historical analysis of prostitution policy, Scoular et al's chapter understands contemporary policy within the wider history of the control and governance of prostitution and sex workers. Subsequently, they also argue that recent constructions of street sex work as a form of anti-social behaviour must be viewed as merely the latest attempt to construct the street sex worker as a social 'other'. They conclude that the alleged antithesis of sex work and community safety can be viewed as arising as much from the ideological operation of law as from any inherent feature of commercial sex. Chapter Three explores the implications for 'community safety' within the broader context of New Labour governance and the potential seeds of transformative possibilities and radical democratic praxis contained within New Labour's approach. While there are a number of potentially positive outcomes in the strategy, for O'Neill, the bottom line is that the complexity of prostitution and the commercial exchange of sex for money has been missed in an attempt to protect communities, manage public space, and on the one hand to regulate off-street work (acknowledged as safer than street-based work) while on the other promoting a zero-tolerance approach to street-based sex work. Drawing on a combination of critical policy analysis and findings from a range of recent research projects, this chapter deconstructs the assumptions about community and safety shaping the policy reforms. From there the chapter explores the contemporary contours of governance shaping New Labour interventions more generally, before using this to explore the exclusion and misrecognition of both the empirical realities of much sex work and the actual individuals involved.

Chapter Four is the first of the chapters that deal with specific issues. In this chapter, Sanders examines the issue of indoor sex work. She claims that the indoor sexual marketplace of brothels, saunas and massage parlours has historically been left to manage itself, with limited intervention from policing agencies. Her chapter goes on to examine the current nature of the indoor sex markets in light of *A Coordinated Prostitution Strategy* and looks critically at the impact of 'disrupting sex markets', and examines the arguments for rejecting a system that regulates indoor sex venues, through licensing for example. She also discusses the proposed changes to the law to enable 'two (or three)' women to work together indoors and the plans to minimise exploitation through an action plan on trafficking. How these objectives translate into practice, and the implications for practitioners and policy are also assessed.

In Chapter Five, Melrose provides a detailed analysis of the reforms in relation to women drug users. She explores the extent to which the recommendations made during the consultation period were incorporated into the prostitution strategy (Home Office, 2006) and reflects on the implications for practice. Melrose argues that the issue of drug use by sex workers cannot be separated from wider social problems experienced by this group, especially poverty. She suggests that the prostitution strategy conflates drug use and sex work, reducing involvement in the latter as a result of the former. By so doing, Melrose argues that the government has absolved itself of responsibility to tackle the underlying conditions that drive women and young people into prostitution and problematic drug use, leading her to argue that the strategy offers only a cheap fix for drug-using sex workers.

In Chapter Six, Whowell and Gaffney provide a similarly detailed examination of the impact of policy reform on one constituency of individuals involved in selling sex – men. They argue that the strategy does indeed focus on the role of men in prostitution, but that the focus is centred on men being abusers of women and children involved in the sex industry, and that as such it vilifies men as the sole perpetrators who drive the sex market. This chapter traces the implications of the strategy for men involved in prostitution and details the manner in which many of the social, health and welfare needs of men in sex work are simply ignored. Of equal concern to Whowell and Gaffney is the way in which tighter regulation and a more punitive approach to prostitution, in the context of male sex workers, can operate to undermine the liberalisation of homosexual sex brought about by the Wolfenden Report.

Chapter Seven turns the focus of discussion onto children and young people. In this chapter Pearce explores some of the inherent contradictions within an analysis of sexual exploitation which, by seeing all young people as victims of abuse, simplifies complex questions about young people's agency and self-determinism. The chapter identifies blind spots in this analysis that have not been fully explored. Pearce's central argument is that while there is no denying the violence and abuse that exists for sexually exploited young people, addressing the issue solely through child protection services misses some of the key social and welfare conditions experienced by many of these young people that make them vulnerable to sexual exploitation.

In Chapter Eight, Morgan Thomas explores policy developments in Scotland, and in particular the introduction of zero tolerance policies towards prostitution and what this means in practice. Morgan Thomas provides her reflections on the politics of prostitution reform in Edinburgh not from an academic perspective, but as someone who has worked within the sex industry for nearly three decades. Her reflections start with a recognition that Edinburgh was a pioneering city in relation to adopting a broader policy of 'zero tolerance' towards violence against women. In the early 1990s, this translated into local policies based on toleration of sex work as a means of ensuring individual sex workers' safety. However, in the space of 10 years, the same broad policy of 'zero tolerance' towards violence against women translated into a fundamentally different set of policies and practices. Now, as the chapter makes clear, criminal justice responses against individuals in the sex industry (sex workers and clients alike) are used as a means of ensuring safety for women by trying to eliminate prostitution. Central to Morgan Thomas's reflections is the distinction between a rhetoric adopted by those advocating the new zero-tolerance-against-prostitution approach and the realities of sex work, violence, exploitation and victimisation (or not) experienced by individual sex workers.

Notes

[1] Metonymy is a figure of speech in which one word is substituted for another as though they signify the same thing.

[2] For a discussion of the links between feminism and prostitution policy around the globe, see Outshoorn (2004).

[3] Source: Office for Criminal Justice Reform, Home Office.

[4] See, for instance, 'Tolerance zones plans in tatters', *Guardian*, 14 December 2005.

TWO

What's anti-social about sex work? Governance through the changing representation of prostitution's incivility

Jane Scoular, Jane Pitcher, Rosie Campbell, Phil Hubbard and Maggie O'Neill

Introduction

Recent reforms of prostitution policy in the UK have been abolitionist in tone, with concerns about community safety and violence against women encouraging zero-tolerance strategies. In relation to street sex work, such strategies include a range of interventions – from voluntary referrals to compulsory intervention orders and Anti-Social Behaviour Orders (ASBOs) designed to extricate women apparently 'trapped' in street prostitution. Despite being heralded as a new approach, we argue that recent constructions of street sex work as a form of anti-social behaviour must be viewed as merely the latest attempt to construct the street sex worker as a social 'other'. In this chapter we utilise both critical and empirical forms of enquiry to uncover the relationship between dominant constructions of the 'problem of prostitution' and the associated norms that operate across various historical epochs, focusing in particular on the recent association between street sex work and anti-social behaviour. By situating this within a critical historical analysis of prostitution policy, we are able to contextualise contemporary policy within the wider history of control and governance in order to show that the alleged antithesis of sex work to community safety owes as much to the ideological operation of law as to any inherent feature of commercial sex. In the main part of the chapter we consider the practical implications of recent reforms, which continue to follow this ideology. By reflecting on our recent Joseph Rowntree Foundation-funded study, which examined the experiences of those living and working in areas of street sex work, we outline some of the dangers of policy frameworks and techniques of control that continue to situate sex work as antithetical to the cultivation of community safety.

Recent reforms

Recent reviews and reforms of prostitution law in the UK (Home Office, 2004; 2006; Scottish Executive, 2004; 2006; 2007 Criminal Justice and Immigration Bill; 2007 Prostitution (Public Places) (Scotland) Act) have been widely acclaimed as marking an important sea-change in sex work policy, with new anxieties about community safety and exploitation joining more long-standing concerns about morality and decency. The Home Office strategy (2006) which informs current law reform proposals prioritises the promotion of community safety and the elimination of street sex work as a form of commercial exploitation in its key objectives. The strategy cites four main objectives, namely: challenging the inevitability of street prostitution; reducing street prostitution; improving the safety and quality of life of the communities affected by street prostitution; and reducing all forms of commercial sexual exploitation.

To achieve these objectives, a dichotomous regulatory regime is proposed which combines a regime of zero tolerance to street sex work alongside a limited (and as yet unspecified) form of selective deregulation of indoor work. While there is little specific content regarding indoor work, the message regarding street sex work is clear: 'Street prostitution is not an activity that we can tolerate in our towns and cities' (Home Office, 2006: 1). The idea that managed areas or tolerance zones might be a pragmatic means of managing street sex work has hence been rejected as endangering both community safety and women's equality, which is thought to be better protected by the increased policing of kerb crawlers and the promotion of multi-agency work designed to help workers quit street sex work. Women's participation in this process of quitting is not voluntary but is to be enforced via compulsory rehabilitation orders proposed under the 2007 Criminal Justice and Immigration Bill. These policy 'shifts' thus represent a significant revision of the abolitionist stance that has characterised UK prostitution policy since the 19th century (Sanders, 2005). However, what remains constant is the ideological construction of street sex work (and the street sex worker) as a problem that threatens the integrity of the social, leading us to question just what is indeed new or radical in the recent reforms and to consider their relationship to dominant modes of governance.

Constructing sex work as a social problem: legacies and antecedents

Theories of social control indicate that the creation of identifiable groups requiring control or regulation is central to the process of maintaining particular forms of social order and preserving dominant forms hegemonic power relations (Cohen, 1972). An important body of critical literature has documented the discursive process involved in the creation of the 'prostitute subject', from the moral panic surrounding the 1864, 1866 and 1869 Contagious Diseases Acts (Walkowitz, 1980; Spongberg, 1997), through to its reconstruction as an issue of public nuisance and penal concern in Wolfenden (Wolfenden Committee Report, 1957) and the subsequent 1959 Street Offences Act (McLeod, 1982; Smart, 1989; Edwards, 1993; 1997; Self, 2003). This work highlights the way in which law makers and enforcers endeavoured to control the 'prostitute' in an attempt to control cultural anxieties over the dynamics of urbanisation and women's shifting roles. Excluding problematic 'others' was and remains central to governments' attempts to secure the public's individual moral and social health (Smart, 1989: 94). The negative consequences for those sex workers excluded from the symbolic and material protection afforded by inclusion into the social (in terms of the diminution of social, political and legal status) is the long-standing legacy of such binary law making.

In a similar vein, contemporary scholarship provides a critical perspective on the recent emphasis on sex work both as a form of anti-social behaviour and as a paradigmatic instance of violence against women, linking these discourses to contemporary forms of governance, specifically New Labour's moral authoritarianism and responsibilisation agenda, which operates through the rhetoric of social inclusion (Phoenix and Oerton, 2005; Scoular and O'Neill, 2007) rather than structural change.

We consider these insights below as we reflect on our recent empirical work, which considers the experience of those living and working in areas of street sex work (Pitcher et al, 2006) and offers an important insight into the costs that accrue from policies that continue to be structured on binaries, in this case between community safety and street sex work.

Street sex work as anti-social and uncivil

Sex workers may often live in the areas where they work, but contemporary policy statements ignore such issues to posit street sex workers as destroying communities. This notion is strengthened by the recent emphasis in public policy on community safety and by the incidence over the past two decades of high-profile neighbourhood protests against street sex work. While some of these campaigns have been short lived, others (notably in Birmingham, Bradford and Cardiff) have been officially sanctioned through community Street Watch programmes, on the basis that street sex work impinges on local quality of life (Hubbard, 1998; Sagar, 2005). Campaigners allege nuisance caused by noisy clients, increased traffic flows, discarded condoms and harassment of local (non-working) women. They also raise specific concerns about the distress that may be caused to women and children confronted with the sights and sounds of sex work. This depiction is repeated in the Home Office strategy, which proposed a new moral framework designed not only to 'save' women and children from exploitation but also to protect communities from 'harassment from kerb-crawlers, prostitution and drug-related litter ... public sex acts and the general degradation of areas used for street prostitution' (Home Office, 2006: 13). There also appears to be a concern among home owners that the presence of sex work compromises their property values, giving an area a reputation for criminality and incivility.

Hubbard (1998) notes the way in which community protesters reproduce particular spatial orders by invoking the language of siege, and which suggests that sex workers are intruding on community space by virtue of their occupation of public (street) spaces. Other issues are raised by such protests, with Sagar (2005) noting that protestors often act on behalf of a small (and retired) section of the community. She also notes that the impact of their zero-tolerance activities has been to displace sex work to neighbouring districts, thus undermining the work of other agencies:

> The Street Watch programme has provided a powerful medium for particular community members to exercise a state-endorsed form of social exclusion against the very members of the community whom they are striving to include. (Sagar, 2005: 108)

This relates to more general critiques of community safety discourse, which suggest that it has become 'a vehicle for intolerance, legitimating the complaints of older, settled members of the community who speak as "consumers of community safety resources"' (Squires, 2006: 3). These campaigns, as Phoenix notes, add a new complexity to the construction of prostitution as a problem 'drawing on more diffuse notions of "public" nuisance' (Phoenix, 2001: 24). Indeed, attempts to define the harms facing communities when street sex work takes place in localities are rarely informed by empirical data. For example, there is little clear evidence that reductions in street sex work are always accompanied by declines in other crimes. In fact, the opposite may often be true, as the presence of sex workers can enhance levels of street surveillance (Hubbard et al, 2006). The dynamics of urban decline and regeneration are also often more complex than statements by authors such as Sion (1977: 15–16) and politicians (Criminal Law Revision Committee, 1985: 14), which link prostitution to neighbourhood, property and business decline. Prostitution's assumed association with crime and fear of crime (Matthews, 1993), which is routinely used to justify increased control, may also be too simplistic, with protesters relying on a circuitous logic that intuitively connects prostitution with vulnerability to crime, even if it is not a crime in itself (Phoenix, 2001: 24). We have argued elsewhere that gentrifiers may exploit divisions between sex workers and other residents in order to create space for redevelopment (Hubbard et al, 2006), increasing sex workers' vulnerability to crime by displacing them to more vulnerable spaces. Such findings concur with studies of community safety initiatives which conclude that these generally operate to maintain established interests; as Hancock (2006) notes, community safety's rhetoric of inclusion conceals its uneven distribution across class and social divisions, increasing, for example, the marginalisation of particular groups, including the young (Brown, 1998; Squires, 1998; Measor and Squires, 2000), ethnic minorities (FitzGerald, 2001) and sexual minorities (McGhee, 2006). Analysis of recent prostitution reforms and the findings of our research, outlined below, also suggest that sex workers are not equal recipients of community safety and will continue to be excluded from resources if dominant understandings of citizenship and sex work continue to be set as an opposable binary.

Yet, despite these critical insights, community protests have been significant factors (along with a growing recognition of violence against women and concern about trafficking) leading to the recent government review, evidenced across a diverse range of documents including *Tackling Street Prostitution: Towards an Holistic Approach*, *Paying the Price*, *A Coordinated Prostitution Strategy* and the Scottish Expert Review *Being Outside*. Across these documents, prostitution is once again anti-socially constructed – referred to as responsible for multiple harms experienced by both women and communities:

> Prostitution makes victims of many of those involved in it, and of those communities in which it takes place. (Home Office, 2004: 19)

Yet within these statements the anti-social nature of street sex work is presented as a self-evident truth, justifying a zero-tolerance approach which includes increased enforcement against kerb crawling, the use of ASBOs and the promotion of 'prevention and exiting interventions' for female sex workers. However, as we will discuss in relation to our empirical findings, such a reductive approach does not reflect communities' diverse and complex experiences of sex work, and leads to blanket policies that are ill matched to the realities of street sex work in many locales: while there may well be conflicts arising from specific incidents, and there are often intolerant community voices within neighbourhoods, it is by no means the case that intolerance is shared by all members of communities (Campbell and Hancock, 1998).

Living in areas of street sex work: evidence from a recent study

A research study undertaken recently for the Joseph Rowntree Foundation as part of its Public Spaces Programme (Pitcher et al, 2006) demonstrates a much greater complexity among community views than is assumed in policy literature. The research was undertaken in five localities (termed Westside, Riverside, Eastside, Southside and Central) and involved interviews with a range of local residents and community and business representatives, street-based sex workers, staff in support projects and other local agencies. The aim of the research was to explore the dynamics within neighbourhoods associated with street sex work, elicit a range of community views and responses and to identify policies that best met the needs of both local residents and sex workers in reducing tension and conflict in areas of sex work. The researchers found a range of community views, and while for many of the residents we interviewed sex work was not considered a major quality of life concern, when compared with other issues such as crime, housing and environmental quality, nonetheless some experienced severe problems. One of the most widespread concerns was that street sex markets impinged on residents' use of public spaces (particularly public parks and alleyways), although it appeared that other factors which were not necessarily related to sex markets, such as drug dealing and drug use, also had a negative impact. The high visibility of sex workers and their clients was also a major concern for some, as well as the detritus associated with sex work, and late-night noise caused by sex workers and their clients. Some residents described feeling fearful of leaving and returning to their homes because of the presence of sex workers and their clients close to their house. Many respondents recounted a different experience, however, some describing how they engaged with women working on the street, sometimes making them cups of tea and giving them food.

A key finding was that community responses seemed to be dependent on the extent to which authorities in the city had taken action to address concerns. For example, one resident in Westside described 'having an unacceptable situation and nobody would listen'; another spoke of activity being 'twenty-four seven' and 'we just couldn't cope with it any more'. A group of residents in this area set up a Street Watch group which patrolled the streets in a van and collected 'evidence of women and the cars they get into or the lorries they get into or whatever' to present to the police. In Riverside, residents also formed street patrols, explaining their involvement (described by one respondent as 'people power') as resulting from the lack of agency responses. There had also been some active campaigning against sex work from residents in Southside. Nonetheless, many residents in these areas did not support street patrolling, with some finding the action 'unpleasant', 'bigoted' and 'distasteful'. In Central and Eastside, while there had been action by residents in the past, currently few complaints were documented. This change appeared to relate to a number of factors, including the development of integrated responses involving a range of partners (including sex-work projects); consultation activities taking place prior to implementation of initiatives; the presence of discrete areas away from people's houses where women were able to work and access services at particular times; and multi-agency alternatives to increased enforcement, such as court diversion schemes.

Diverse views of residents

While some residents were morally opposed to sex work per se, a majority did not share this view. Views ranged from extreme intolerance, through modest intolerance and modest tolerance to proactive tolerance, with most respondents holding views in the middle of the two extremes.[1] These categories were not mutually exclusive and we found some respondents who expressed the full range of views during a single interview. For example, one resident, who was active in a street patrol group, spoke of prostitutes and pimps as being 'ghastly people' and talked of the degree of 'hurt and upset' that sex work brought to communities, supporting Anti-Social Behaviour Orders as a mechanism to be used to control sex workers, with the main concern being that they should be moved out of the area. Later on in the interview, this individual described a sex worker she had encountered as a 'really nice woman … not a horrible person', expressed concern for some of the younger women she had seen on the street, and was 'horrified' at the gaps in service provision in terms of both prevention and initiatives to support women leaving prison: 'We're not helping them an awful lot are we?'

Within the typology described above, there was also a wide range of views. For example, those residents who could be described as tolerant had different reasons for this standpoint, often perceiving sex workers according to popular stereotypes. For some, sex workers were victims, exploited and vulnerable:

> I do feel sorry for the girls because they are under sort [sic] of people in charge of them. I've heard that they have to earn a certain amount of money to give back to their minders and whatever. The minders have got them into this trap and it's very difficult for the girls to get out of this trap because they're reliant on drugs. They're hooked on drugs, they're reliant on drugs and they don't have any choice but to go out onto the streets and earn money for their drugs. (Resident, Eastside)

Others, while displaying sympathy, saw the women as degraded and deserving of pity:

> It's just sad that they are in a situation that they have to sell themselves on the street. To even contemplate that, you have to have sunk pretty low. (Resident, Central)

To some residents, sex work was 'not a problem':

> Really for me it hasn't been a problem. I don't see that as a problem. The girls actually come in and most are polite. They come in, they buy what they want and then go. I don't normally have any problem with the girls. It's, they're normally okay. (Resident and shop manager, Southside)

Several expressed concerns for the safety of sex workers, mainly because, as one Riverside resident expressed it, 'it's a dangerous occupation'. We also came across many instances where residents had had social interactions with sex workers on a regular basis, for example as neighbours, as customers of local shops or restaurants, as mothers of children at the local school, or simply smiling at them and saying 'hello' on the street. One respondent in Westside recounted a story of a friend who had been so offended by the actions of the street patrols that she started 'taking cups of tea' out to the women.

The majority of residents displayed views situated at the mid-point of the typology, in that they were sympathetic towards the sex workers in their area, but also wanted the negative impacts to be addressed appropriately by the authorities.

> I think there's such a range of reasons why women may end up doing that work that I don't think it's my position to say they should or shouldn't be doing it. But I think there's appropriate places and inappropriate places for it to happen. But I think they need a degree of protection. I think people sharing the space with them need some protection too. It's trying to find a route through it all that, you know, compromises on both sides where it could actually coexist. (Resident, Riverside)

For those who presented a lack of sympathy to sex workers, there were also different reasons given. For example, for one resident in Southside it was a matter of territory:

> I think we didn't know them in the area. If they lived in my street then I don't think I would have said anything to them, but because it was a territorial thing. These people have come into your area and they're standing there and they're not going to move.

For this person and some other residents, it was also because they had been brought up to believe that sex workers were immoral or evil (although in some cases their views had changed with experience). Some respondents had formed their views as a result of their experiences, for example being abused by some sex workers or their clients, or witnessing sexual activities. Others felt that sex work brought crime into the area, or that the presence of sex markets devalued local property. At the more extreme end of intolerance, some residents saw sex work as only bringing harm to communities, and associated sex workers with uncleanliness and disease:

> All they do is contribute violence, kerb crawling, drugs. Everything about prostitution is negative, especially the ones who are here. From a health perspective they are a health hazard. They take drugs and use needles and the needles are left for starters ... many are drug abusers in this area, they pose a community health threat. (Resident, Central)

We encountered different moral perspectives on sex work and sex workers that influenced people's views on how the issues should be dealt with. For example, for some, sympathy was conditional on a certain type of behaviour or attitude, particularly on being receptive to receiving help. Some residents differentiated between the reasons for working, with working for a 'loaf of bread' apparently being more acceptable than doing the same thing to support 'a drug habit'. While for some, sex work was seen as a bad thing, for a few individuals the sex workers themselves were seen as evil, not part of the 'law-abiding, honest majority'. Not all moral views were negative, however. In some cases respondents stressed that 'people have the right to choose what to do' and several residents spoke of 'not judging people'. Contrary to assumptions made by some participants about the relative tolerance levels of particular ethnic groups (with some white residents, for example, voicing their opinion that Muslim communities would not be accepting of sex workers), we found the same range of perspectives within different ethnic groups.

Differing perspectives also reflected the extent to which sex workers were seen as individuals rather than in terms of a stereotype. To a minority, they were not perceived as rational beings, capable of responding to the concerns of others or participating in society:

> The prostitutes are not discreet. They're noisy, they're shouting, they're screaming. (Resident, Westside)

> And there was no point in trying to reason with them because there was no reasoning involved. They were high on drugs. They were out of their heads. They were unreasonable. So you know, the idea that this industry could coexist in a community is, from our experience, it just doesn't work because you're not dealing with rational people or with people who care. (Resident, Riverside)

Other residents recognised that there was diversity among sex workers, in the same way as among other members of the population, and some stressed the need to see sex workers primarily as people rather than as a category:

> Because at the end of the day they're human beings. And they've got ... their lives are different to ours you know. So that's how I see people. And I think if that's the way those people want to live, and that's a way of earning money. (Resident, Southside)

Views on enforcement measures

The role of sex-work projects and other agencies was also a contributing factor to building relations between sex workers and residents. All of the case study areas had funded projects working with sex workers from a harm-reduction perspective, some of which undertook mediation in the neighbourhoods where street sex work took place. In some locales, staff in other public agencies, such as community wardens, also engaged in mediation activities. Environmental initiatives, such as clearing debris and foliage from public spaces in order to make them more accessible and increase safety, also featured in some neighbourhoods; police crackdowns on sex work still featured in most areas. As one agency representative in Southside commented: 'Enforcement is easier, it's cheaper and it's tangible. It can be seen to be effective. Whereas all of the other areas are very hard work, intense work, its financial implications.' However, there was considerable variation of the use of ASBOs, CRASBOs and other civil measures against sex workers in our study, ranging from only two for specific instances of anti-social behaviour in Central, to what might be termed 'blanket use' against sex workers in Westside, where the authorities had responded to calls by an active group of residents for stricter enforcement

For some residents, the merits of ASBOs were clear. For example, one resident described them as 'very effective' in moving the women on, and another as 'brilliant ... in the sense that for the first time there was something that we felt we could do'. Although the ASBOs were seen as offering rapid respite from the problems, these residents did acknowledge that their main effect was to move sex workers into adjacent areas or other cities in the vicinity, as well as acting as barriers to sex workers accessing outreach and support services. Others were cynical about the long-term effects:

> at the end of the day, it is not solving the individual's problem, they're still gonna breach the ASBO because

they're still gonna need the money. So it's only ... It's just a step to prison really, isn't it. It's almost inevitable that they will end up in prison as a result. (Resident, Central)

In this sense, some residents were opposed to the use of ASBOs generally, whereas others felt that while there might be circumstances in which they would be acceptable, they were disproportionate to the problems in relation to street sex work:

In theory I think you need some kind of measure to take against the kind of people who persistently disrupt the local community but they should be fairly exceptional. In my head they would normally be aimed at kind of teenage boys, kind of gangs of boys hanging around who are violent. I don't think it's at all appropriate to use them on street workers ... it really should be for people who are actually damaging property or other people. (Resident, Riverside)

But I think an anti-social behaviour order says to me that is [someone] that is making someone's life horrendous and I don't think working girls make people's lives horrendous. They can be annoying because of what's happening but I don't think it ruins your life to the extent of what the ASBOs should be [for]. (Resident, Eastside)

The suggestion here is that many residents interviewed saw the wider picture and displayed understanding and sympathy towards the women.

ASBOs were seen by agency and project staff as bringing more women into the criminal justice system, increasing their vulnerability:

It doesn't solve the problem. And again I would rather see the girls being helped than just being criminalised even more. Which is what all these things in the ASBO do. Again it moves the girls on ... you get one in [one area] and then you get one in [another area] and then you go into different areas. What does it do for the girls? It doesn't do anything for them. I would much rather see them educated or helped to be able to get out of what they're stuck in rather than being further and further criminalised. (Resident, Westside)

Similarly, support projects expressed concerns about the impact of ASBOs on women's safety:

> The locations [of working] have moved a bit because of more police activity and ASBOs. I'm concerned that women are more vulnerable. They are being pushed towards [another neighbourhood], which is less residential, dark, less safe. Some residents are concerned that that puts women more at risk, although others are happy that the problem is gone. (Agency representative, Eastside)

Sex workers themselves did not understand why they were being penalised by the new measures, particularly since many of the women we interviewed endeavoured as far as possible to work away from people's houses and minimise disruption to local residents.

> When I got the ASBO, I thought … anti-social behaviour orders were for bad neighbours and residents and things like that and I was like, I'm not a bad neighbour – know what I mean? I've never had any hassle with my neighbours. That was the first thing I thought…. I've kept myself to myself. (Sex worker, Riverside)

> …because [when I got the ASBO] they were saying I was a nuisance to residents and everything. But I've never caused no trouble or nothing. I was never badmouthed, I've never done mouthing or be gobby or anything … because I never used to stand outside people's houses and everything because it ain't very nice. So I would make sure I weren't by any houses or anything. (Sex worker, Southside)

Alternatives to enforcement-led approaches

Some respondents felt that sex work was incompatible with residential areas. Suggestions for alternatives that would move sex work away from residential neighbourhoods included designated areas in non-residential sites and moving sex workers into other forms of sex work, particularly indoor-based work. Indoor working was considered by many to be a safer option, but there were seen to be barriers for street sex workers which limited their ability to move into indoor establishments. Many indoor venues have strict regulations about drug use on the premises.

There is also seen to be a hierarchy, with on-street workers being perceived by some indoor workers as lower in status:

> They're not allowed to [move into saunas]. They try to work from their own houses, like I have, but unless you're really clean and nobody knows you worked on the street, you're all right, but if they know you used to be a street girl they just think you're trashy, because 'I'll do it for sixty pound whereas you'll do it for a tenner'. To them you're trashy. And they won't let you in with drugs. (Sex worker, Westside)

Some people sounded a cautionary note about the apparent relative safety of moving into indoor-based work. This was not necessarily a safer option, particularly for women who were drug dependent and who would not be able to work in an establishment, but might start working on their own or with friends from a house or flat. For example, a resident in Southside pointed to the fact that women might be more vulnerable to exploitation and isolated from services in some indoor locations. This concern was echoed by project workers in Eastside and Riverside, although there had been situations where the project was able to keep in touch with women moving off the street and 'put the safety aspect' into their work (project worker, Eastside).

Respondents also discussed alternative policies that moved away from primarily enforcement-led approaches. One alternative seen as effective by agencies and residents alike in two of the case study areas was the use of court diversion schemes. These schemes were not premised on unrealistic notions of 'exiting'; rather, the main conditions were that women arrested for soliciting or loitering should engage with the local sex-work project for two sessions (Aris and Pitcher, 2004; Hunter and May, 2004). Although participants in the scheme did not have to make a commitment for further engagement with services, in reality engagement does continue for many women, but on their terms. The role of sex-work projects has been central in this process, building up trust over a long period of time (often several years), helping women to get to a stage when they are ready to address some of the problems they face.

The research study also found that antipathetic views of residents towards sex workers can be changed, particularly through initiatives such as community mediation and awareness raising. Here the role of sex-work projects (and also other agents such as community wardens and even the police) is central. For example, in one of the case study areas (Eastside) the local sex-work project has acted as an intermediary between residents and sex workers, addressing problems in a constructive way that involves both residents and sex workers as agents. Residents interviewed were very positive about the work of the sex-work project and the steps it had taken to address their concerns by communicating them to sex workers (many of whom also lived locally). For instance, where women were soliciting outside schools and a local mosque, which was clearly of serious concern to many residents, the project was able to discuss these concerns with sex workers in the locality and persuade them to work in a different location. As a result, residents had become much more sympathetic to the needs of local sex workers and had even expressed their concern, during the Home Office consultation (*Paying the Price*), that the welfare of the sex workers should be taken into account in any future policy. As we will consider below, it seems that such an inclusive approach has not been taken up by the Home Office.

Tackling exploitation or widening the net of control?

In contrast to our findings, which suggest some potential for coexistence, the new UK prostitution strategy appears reluctant to include sex workers as citizens, among other groups. Despite references to community involvement 'in the development of an effective local response to prostitution' (Home Office, 2006: 18) and to 'strong partnership[s] with the police, support services and the community' (Home Office, 2006: 15), community participation, the Home Office strategy and local authority guidance in Scotland continue to exclude the voices and interests of sex workers. This makes it difficult to imagine how they can participate, except in their own exclusion.

The recent focus on exiting does little to help this. The strategy has a four-staged approach which features increasing levels of compulsion: from an initial voluntary referral to support projects, to pre-charge diversion, then drug testing following a charge, and finally to prosecution through the criminal justice system for those who 'persist'. The latter includes the use of ASBOs. Despite substantial criticism of the ASBO route (Gil-Robles, 2004; Home Office, 2004; Sanders, 2004; Scottish Executive, 2004; London Assembly, 2005; Millie et al, 2005; Rowlands, 2005; Pitcher et al, 2006), the Home Office strategy does not propose lessening the use of ASBOs, but simply tacks it on as an additional 'intervention order'. While there is an element of voluntarism in this approach to policing, it is clear that if women are not ready to 'reform', the next stage of compulsory rehabilitation will follow soon after. This renders the notion of voluntarism highly questionable in this context. Here we see familiar contradictions within policy documents which emphasise that sex workers are not criminals, while the policies effectively criminalise them by identifying them as a source of anti-sociality. While seemingly contradictory, this is simply evidence of what Sullivan (2001) terms schizophrenic criminal justice: a duality evidenced by the coexistence of socially inclusive neoliberal techniques of regulation and more overt forms of control and repression. Inclusion has no intrinsic value but is utilised as a feature of risk management and responsibilisation. As Garland (1997: 6) notes, inclusion is contingent on offender change and compliance, and when it fails it can be quickly substituted by more effective means such as custody and incapacitation. Hence, current proposals, by offering inclusion only to those who responsibly exit and adopt 'normal' life-styles, continue the hegemonic moral and political regulation of sex workers (Scoular and O'Neill, 2007). It is interesting to note that the Scottish Expert Review *Being Outside*, instigated after the failure of the Tolerance Zones Bill, did include a number of reforms which offered greater recognition to the citizenship rights of sex workers and attempted some balance of their safety with that of the wider community. This included: a commitment to a minimum level of services for sex workers (not contingent upon exiting); caution against using ASBOs except as a last resort and after packages of support had been available; using enforcement within an overall strategy to reduce nuisance, which involved some corporate responsibility on the part of local authorities to plan for sex work; and proposals to remove the status-based nature of soliciting and to require actual proof of annoyance. However, the political manoeuvring and the increasing hegemonic understanding of sex work as violence against women (rooted in radical feminist understandings of power and sexuality (see Scoular, 2004)) that followed has meant that the potential of reforms in Scotland has been lost in the 2007 Prostitution (Public Places) (Scotland) Act. Proposals that attempted to move some way towards reconciling sex workers' rights with community interests have been interpreted as 'tolerating prostitution' and have been abandoned in preference for a model based on criminalising men and framed by rhetorical commitments to addressing the victimised status of women involved in street sex work, in line with the more limited visions of the Home Office strategy.

However, these forms of control may be even more extensive than first imagined. The strategy not only maintains the criminalisation of soliciting but also recommends rehabilitative interventions for 'those individuals who, for whatever reason, continue to be involved in street prostitution' (Home Office, 2006: 42). Thus, the previous regime of criminalisation is reframed and augmented by a wider range of control mechanisms and forms of professional intervention that may be even more pervasive than the previous fines and/or cautions system, with increased 'protection' mirrored in the greater policing of women's lives (Phoenix, 2002: 82). The ideology underpinning previous forms of regulation thus continues via the focus on exiting as a means of reducing community harm and the exploitation of women; in effect, the problem is reduced to 'one of recalcitrant individuals unwilling to accept offers of "help and support"' (Melrose, 2006a: 12). This promotes a form of governance that individualises problems and detracts attention from the state, which is absolved from tackling the underlying conditions that give rise to prostitution in the first place (Scoular and O'Neill, 2007), such as women's and young persons' poverty and social exclusion (Phoenix and Oerton, 2005; Melrose, 2006a: 12). As Scoular and O'Neill argue:

> in the name of 'protecting victims and communities', the state simultaneously removes itself from any role in the processes of social exclusion of women who sell sex while extending its control over subjects. In so doing, it re-presents itself as not only the protective force against a demonized and distant organized 'sex trade' (tough on crime and the causes of crime) and the increasingly criminalized client, but also as the facilitator of exit and support to those re-classified (and not all are) as victims. The state's role in structural exclusion and in perpetuating norms of the sex industry is thus masked by the progressive governance of sex work. (Scoular and O'Neill, 2007: 769)

Despite a number of recommendations to treat sex workers as vulnerable witnesses and to improve the prosecution of crimes against them, and by offering recognition only to those who can fulfil the criteria set by a post-victim identity, the proposals fail to address the vulnerability that arises from the continued criminalisation of soliciting. Indeed they serve to exacerbate this by adopting a zero-tolerance approach, which means that those unable to exit (often the most vulnerable) will face further exclusion and marginalisation.

Conclusion

In this chapter we have argued that, by continuing to frame sex work as antithetical to public order, under a new discourse of anti-sociality, recent reforms perpetuate the marginalisation of street sex work. By starting from a 'zero tolerance' perspective, the policy immediately disenfranchises one of the main stakeholders – the sex worker; yet this continued focus on control of crime and disorder does not ensure – and may indeed imperil – the safety of those most vulnerable. By failing to reconcile sex workers' *in situ* rights and safety within a discourse of community safety, the reforms actually undermine any commitment to tackle exploitation, and the rhetoric of 'community safety' merely becomes a lever for increased control. Nor does it encourage good relations and coexistence, given that a more communitarian-focused understanding of community safety would be required to achieve this (Hancock, 2006: 212).

Yet, as our research indicates, the potential exists within our cities for a more supportive relationship to develop between sex workers and communities. To support this, we argue that it is important to develop policies that take a more holistic, multi-stakeholder approach to addressing the issues, taking into account the needs of different groups, including residents and sex workers (who themselves are sometimes residents). The approach in Eastside works well locally, but needs to be supported at senior policy level in order to be sustainable more widely. It requires a national policy that recognises the need for alternative interventions beyond those that seek simply to expel sex work, increasing the social exclusion of an already marginalised group. Such a sustained approach is best supported by a policy framework that overcomes the antithesis between sex worker and society – a binary that has defined and bedevilled prostitution policy for centuries. It is thus to be hoped that more complex and inclusive understandings of citizenship will develop, so that some degree of coexistence between residents and sex workers becomes the norm, not the exception.

Note
[1] For further details of the typology of residents' views, see Pitcher et al (2006).

THREE

Community safety, rights, redistribution and recognition: towards a coordinated prostitution strategy?

Maggie O'Neill

A coordinated prostitution strategy?

In response to a review of prostitution legislation (the first for 50 years) the Home Office published *A Coordinated Prostitution Strategy* in January 2006, setting out the government's proposals for a strategy focusing predominantly on: prevention of involvement; fostering routes out; and protecting communities from street-based sex markets. Prostitution is defined as 'commercial sexual exploitation' and the strategy seeks to address this issue by: tackling demand via 'disrupting the market' and 'deterring punters'; ensuring justice, by strengthening and enforcing the law against those who exploit and abuse women, young people and children; and tolerating off-street prostitution where two to three women are working together in the interests of their safety. To ensure that the strategy is actioned, there is a focus upon partnerships, the coordination of welfarist policing, and enforcement of the law to divert, deter and rehabilitate those women who do not choose to exit as the most 'responsible' option (see Phoenix and Oerton (2005) and Scoular and O'Neill (2007) for a full discussion of responsibilisation to exit).

In the previous consultation document, *Paying the Price*, the [then] Home Secretary, David Blunkett, located the issues of prostitution in the context of wider policy making and the promotion of civic renewal and community safety (Home Office, 2004: 4). This chapter explores the strategy and discusses its implications for 'community safety' within the broader context of New Labour governance and the potential seeds of transformative possibilities and radical democratic praxis contained within New Labour's approach.

There are a number of potentially positive outcomes in the strategy documented under 'action for government' and 'action for partnerships': a focus on strengthening approaches to child exploitation by ensuring a holistic approach that includes work with schools; including 'communities' through consultation processes like community conferencing; expanding court diversion and reforming the soliciting law; expanding the Ugly Mugs scheme through Crime Stoppers; recruiting police liaison officers; and developing action planning on trafficking. And, importantly, a number of critiques are emerging that seek to foster dialogue and hope to impact upon national policy making, including the shape that the strategy takes in action. Summarising these critiques, the bottom line appears to be that the complexity of the issue has been missed in an attempt to protect communities, manage public space, and on the one hand regulate off-street work (acknowledged as safer than street-based work) while on the other hand promoting a zero-tolerance approach to on-street work. The lack of detail in the strategy leaves many unanswered questions. Melrose argues that 'in the process of consultation, the government appears to have given greater weight to some responses than to others, thus the "new" strategy is not very new at all' and that 'the government has missed an important opportunity to radically rethink its approach to prostitution' (Melrose, 2006a: 4). Moreover, facilitating off-street working, by allowing two to three women (or men) to work together in the interests of safety ignores the variation in off-street working, and the ensuing problems of policing such a wide range of premises, from rooms in dilapidated flats and tenements, to drug dens, to the '"classier" end of the working flat market' (Melrose, 2006a: 15). With a focus squarely upon routes out, the strategy ignores routes in and the structural basis for entry into selling sex (Melrose, 2006a: 19).

Critics also argue that the strategy ignores important health and human rights issues and so 'will not, therefore, tackle genuine areas of vulnerability and exploitation' (Boynton and Cusick, 2006: 191). It is argued by Boynton and Cusick that multi-agency work by healthcare professionals will be disrupted if red light areas are phased out, and this will increase the risks to sex workers, reduce collaborative working practices and impact on basic health and safety. Drawing on Kinnell's (2006) research, the authors state that 87 sex workers have been murdered since 1990. The endemic nature of violence against sex workers, and against women in general, is a vital area to be taken up by the coordinated strategy and is supported by an enormous amount of research by feminists (Hanmer and Saunders, 1984; Kelly, 1988; Hanmer et al, 1989; O'Neill, 1996; Sanders, 2005; Kinnell, 2006). 'The prostitute's status as "other", operating illegally or at the margins of legality, reinforces her "throwaway" status and in relation to violence against her she is seen as a deserving victim' (Bland, 1982). This has serious implications for social policy and is an issue that needs to be addressed in all its complexity. Moreover, a focus upon partnerships, the coordination of welfarist policing and the enforcement of the law to divert, deter and rehabilitate those women who do not choose to exit as the most 'responsible' option simply sustains the binaries between good/bad, deserving/undeserving women/victims and denies women's agency.

Thus the current national coordinated strategy on prostitution helps to frame street-based prostitution within a discourse of moral and political marginalisation, and the addition of a discourse of zero tolerance plays a major role in the marginalisation of women who sell sex, while also helping to 'create a social milieu in which violence can flourish' (Lowman, 2000: 1009). In mapping out the contours of what he calls the 'discourse of disposal' Lowman maintains that legal structures promote victimisation; prostitution takes place in illicit markets; there is convergence with other illegal markets; and together this alienates prostitutes from protective sources/forces.

What we must also remember is that selling sex takes place within the context of wider social processes and structures, such as global capitalism, consumerism, the growth of a broader sex industry that makes huge revenues, and the feminisation of poverty. People make choices, but not always in conditions of their own choosing.[1] What this means, effectively, is that in the interests of safety and challenging violence, zero-tolerance approaches actually offer little in the way of preventing violence against women, because any attempts to create the conditions for holistic social justice and cultural citizenship are seen as condoning sex work. Zero tolerance is therefore antithetical to social justice for street sex workers.

In the Home Office strategy, the identity of 'the prostitute' is fixed along a victim trajectory that ignores the wealth of research documenting the subjecthood of female and male sex workers. Thus, the prostitute identity is prioritised over other 'ordinary' identities such as worker, mother, sister, daughter, carer, lover, as well as structural, social and gender inequalities that lead to routes in; and this reinforces the prostitute as 'other'. This status as objectified 'other' has important consequences, such as a lack of recognition and being treated as a pariah, as the end-stop in discourses on good women, situated in marginal spaces and places, and a victim of male violence. Media messages provide a particularly powerful symbolic representation of the sex worker as 'other' that feeds into the public imagination, such as 'polluting' or 'contaminating' streets/areas, and street sex markets are variously named as 'capital of vice' / 'street of shame' and responses are named as 'anti-vice campaigns' or 'police clampdowns' (see O'Neill et al, 2000).

Responses to this 'othering' by some feminists, sex-worker support projects and activists is to focus on the *recognition* of women as workers, as sex workers (Bindman and Doezema, 1997), highlighting the temporary nature of the exchange between woman and client as 'labour'. The work of the UK Network of Sex Work Projects (UKNSWP) and the GMB union serves to reinforce the basic premise that 'prostitutes' are 'sex workers' and that reform should address the identity of sex workers within the context of European and international labour law. Thus, sex worker rights and unionisation are a key step on the road to recognition of the sex worker's identity as 'worker', and thus a temporal and not a fixed identity. Unlike most citizens, the identity of the sex worker is wrapped up in what she does, and what she does becomes who she is, regardless of whether she is shopping, socialising, or taking her kids to school. Claims to recognition are therefore an important aspect of work in this area since the late 1970s that has been ignored by the Home Office and the coordinated strategy, which instead see the 'prostitute' through the lens of 'victim' of 'commercial sexual exploitation'.

Barriers to a holistic strategy for prostitution reform

In this chapter, I will argue that there are two major barriers that prevent both imagining and actioning an inclusive, holistic strategy for prostitution reform in the UK that incorporates both rights, redistribution and recognition (see also Fraser, 2000, and Young, 1990) and impacts upon perceptions of community safety. First, the image and representation of 'the prostitute' as an 'other' in certain research, government policy, rhetoric, media representations and, inevitably, the public imagination. The abject status of the sex worker reinforces her position as the end-stop in discourses on normative concepts of womanhood (O'Neill, 2001). Related to this is the terrible reality of violence against sex workers, and that this is understood and represented by some sections of the media as deserving (see Kinnell, 2006). John Lowman (2000) shows very clearly that a 'discourse of disposal' operates in relation to women who sell sex and that their identity as sex workers reinforces notions of 'deserving' victim.

We do need to engage in a process of *recognition* through inclusion of sex workers and projects in research, debates and dialogue (something I have argued and practised for almost two decades now), but we also need to address the issue of *redistribution*, poverty, structural/economic routes in, as well as *rights* such as citizenship rights.

The bottom line from research evidence is that money is at the heart of routes into sex work. In a recent report from New Zealand, where sex work was decriminalised in the 2003 Prostitution Reform Act, the Prostitution Law Review Committee's report work carried out by the Christchurch School of Medicine and Victoria University's Crime and Justice Research Centre found that '93 percent of sex workers cited money as the reason for getting into and staying in the sex industry' (New Zealand Press Association, 2008: 1) and:

> the most significant barriers to exiting are loss of income, reluctance to lose the flexible working hours available in the sex industry and the camaraderie and sense of belonging that some sex workers describe. (New Zealand Press Association, 2008: 1)

Second, current responses by the Home Office to prostitution are inevitably linked to a much broader shift to intolerance and greater punitiveness in Western societies, defined by Phoenix and Oerton (2005) as 'the new moral authoritarianism' (see also Pratt, 1999; Garland, 2001; Scoular and O'Neill, 2007). However, New Labour governance does, I argue, offer both a barrier to inclusive prostitution reform and the seeds for radical reform, incorporating both rights and recognition.

I suggest that any strategic response should focus on the complexity of sex work in the UK in the 21st century and that understanding complexity in order to improve the situation of women and men involved in selling sex be based upon the following key tenets: inclusion, rights, recognition, respect and redistribution. To progress this vision it is important to create the space for women's voices by using inclusive research methodologies, such as Participatory Action Research (PAR), that necessarily create safe spaces for dialogue with sex workers as well as with residents in communities affected by on- and off-street sex work.

Ultimately, what I am suggesting is a politics of inclusion (following the usage of this term by Janet Newman in 2003) informed by a politics of feeling (O'Neill, 2001) that brushes against the grain of the new punitiveness and moral authoritarianism, and reconnects with radical feminist perspectives on violence against women from the perspective of women's lived experience (not government agendas) and includes rights, redistribution and recognition (Fraser, 2000). A politics of inclusion highlights the need to address the cultural citizenship of sex workers and promotes social justice.[2] Social justice is constituted by the interrelation of cultural justice through recognition; distributive justice via equality of opportunity, unionisations, rights under labour law; and associational justice, involving patterns of association and inclusion (O'Neill et al, 2004; 2008). The work of the UKNSWP (chaired by Rosie Campbell) and the National Working Group for Sexually Exploited Children and Young People (chaired by Jenny Pearce) are two examples of national (European and linked to international) networks promoting associational justice for women, men and also young people selling sex (Pearce et al, 2003).

Defining community safety

In 2000, Rosie Campbell and I were commissioned by Walsall South Health Action Zone to undertake a PAR approach to examine prostitution in Walsall. In the Walsall study we found the following community safety concerns expressed by the sex workers we interviewed. Overwhelmingly, the pivotal issue that emerged was how susceptible they are to violence from clients as well as passers-by, and how few *rights* they have as a 'common prostitute'. The following three women raise similar concerns.

> They think you've got no rights. In the papers it will say 'a prostitute' has been murdered. Does it matter that she's a prostitute, she's dead? She is a woman too.

> It was being a mum as well, I thought what would they do if I was murdered, so I came off the streets.

> Nine out of ten times you can always suss them out ... dodgy punters ... you might have seen them before in the area.

Zero tolerance of street prostitution will not address the endemic nature of violence against sex workers – it will merely remove it (to a degree) from public spaces and make it even more risky and unsafe for women who continue selling sex on the street.

Residents in our Walsall study focused on the following issues with regard to community safety. A resident in Focus Group 5 gave a list of the concerns she had:

No safety, harassment, being asked for business, explaining things to children and making up lies to protect them. You can't walk out in a night at all now because someone might come up to you, a client or something and they might say this and that so you can't; you don't feel safe walking anymore.

Two other residents focused on related aspects of community safety:

Greater feeling of intimidation and fear ... they are more in our face now.

It has invaded our homes.

I think there's more chance of ... rather than violence against you yourself on the streets, there's more chance of your home being raided, broken into in that way, than the safety aspect. I think there's a greater degree of break-ins.

Additionally, some residents expressed concern for the safety of sex workers. There was particular concern about vulnerable people involved in sex work and the violence they experienced from pimps and kerb crawlers. Many residents assumed that there were high levels of violence against the women involved and were concerned about this. Residents made suggestions about responding to this issue, which we incorporated into our recommendations.

A minority of the residents we interviewed were aware of the issues which lead women and young people to be involved, but were so angry and frustrated by their current situation that they did not want to focus on routes into sex work and welfare responses to prostitutes. For them, to do so would serve to take the emphasis off their experiences and their feelings of being the victims of sex work.

'Community' concerns are the focal point of the Home Office strategy. In an attempt in part to address 'community' concerns, the Home Office funded research in 2004 conducted by Hester and Westmarland. The researchers found that community mediation and liaison models could have some success in addressing community concerns. In a recent chapter (O'Neill and Campbell, 2006), Rosie and I go on to argue that more constructive and inclusive consultation, including mediation and liaison models, is required to develop policies and practices that may promote civic renewal and active citizenship. A good example of this is the flowering of multi-agency fora/partnership working in the 1990s that incorporated sex worker voices through support projects, as well as directly in some cases, such as the pioneering POW (Prostitute Outreach Workers) project in Nottingham. Research I conducted using the principles of PAR in 1989–90 led to the setting up of a multi-agency forum[3] on which sex workers were represented alongside magistrates, police, the probation service, the health authority, Nottingham University and Nottingham Trent University. The forum facilitated early work by POW to build bridges with magistrates and police and supported the development of an Options project funded by European Social Fund monies, employing an ex-sex worker and running employment and training fairs as well as providing resources for women to pay for childcare and attend courses at local colleges. Residents' representatives were invited to attend the forum, but they declined.

A major barrier to radical change, identified by Adam Crawford, is that the present government's nostalgic appeal to a homogeneous notion of 'community' is incongruous with the radical transformations necessary to realise modern institutions of governance through partnerships' (Crawford, 1997: 74). As our research in Walsall highlighted, communities are marked not by homogeneity but by contingency and diversity, and a broad range of tolerance to street-based sex workers exists alongside resistance and fear of crime, and community safety. Participation in local governance through dialogue, a voice, to be listened to by the responsible authorities and to share in local decision making was what our resident participants wanted most. And to an extent the needs of residents (communities) is a central aspect of the Home Office strategy. However, as noted above, sex workers are marked in the strategy document by their absence.

Beyond labels?

The Home Office strategy effectively defines sex work as no more than a matter of violence and exploitation, and 'community' as something both outside the women selling sex and homogeneous. The complex impact upon women's lives of poverty, history, economics, consumerism and globalisation is negated. We need a strategy that offers fairness and equity to women, men and young people; a balanced approach based on dialogue, communication and ultimately produced in participation with *all* those involved. There are no easy answers or solutions, but a good place to start would be to commission research that develops the suggestions in the strategy for community conferencing and links these to research using participatory methods in order to promote the (radical) principles of progressive governance, as espoused in Janet Newman's (2003) more optimistic version of New Labour governance.

Governance

Governance theory (Kooiman, 1993; Clarke and Newman, 1997; Gamble, 2000; Rhodes, 2000; Newman, 2003; Clarke, 2004) helps us to understand the relationships between the public, private and voluntary sectors; the changing role and power of the state; and the role, experiences and expectations of citizens and communities (Newman, 2003: 15). Newman identifies in New Labour's 'Third Way' a significant shift from governance through hierarchy and competition to governance through networks and partnerships, with an emphasis on inclusion; and that this more holistic approach to governance 'results in the dissolution of old hierarchies and power blocs' (Newman, 2003: 3). Governments, it is argued,

> can no longer achieve their goals through traditional methods of control because of their dependence on a wide range of actors across the public, private and voluntary sectors. They are increasingly obliged to govern at a distance by influencing, persuading and providing incentives for action. At the same time they are developing stronger roles in building partnerships, steering and coordinating, and providing system-wide integration and regulation. New patterns of governance have become more significant, not only because of the fragmentation of the public domain but also because of the growing complexity of social problems and the changing nature of civil society. (Newman, 2003: 16)

Importantly, Newman tells us that the new governance (state–society interaction) depends on systems of co-arrangements that include co-steering, collaboration, and cooperation that in turn depend on new systems of patronage, which in turn raise a number of issues. For example, in seeking to 'empower' people or communities, questions about who are and are not 'included' are raised and issues of tokenism and incorporation go unresolved. Newman's analysis identifies New Labour's policies as constituted by a complex mix of different forms and styles of governing and that this poses challenges to the scope and focus of equality policy and practice. The strong, centralised control over both the party and public services suggests, for Newman, 'a continuing theme of hierarchical governance. Labour is also a strongly managerial administration, emphasising the search for "what works" and unrolling a range of "modernising" policy reforms' (Newman, 2003: 17).

Newman concedes that:

> networks and partnerships do represent an attempt to deal with the complexity of many areas of public policy and incapacity of hierarchical governing to deliver long-term, sustainable policy outcomes. (Newman, 2003: 20)

One way forward, for Newman, is to identify a new research agenda to explore both 'politics of inclusion' and exclusion in the new forms of governance, *and* the 'politics of representation' in the drive to open up decision making and stimulate democratic renewal.

I suggest in a later section (and in earlier work) that participatory methodologies, including mediation and community conferencing (both the latter are included in the Home Office strategy), within the context of critical cultural criminology using qualitative, ethnographic, action-oriented research (that has been conducted by researchers in this area for decades) provide a very good basis for fostering a radical democratic present in policy and practice that demonstrates a politics of inclusion and representation through both redistribution and recognition. 'The opening up of organisations to greater influence by users, citizens and communities – including community activists and politicised user groups – can be a major impetus for change' at the same time as a 'strong possibility of the incorporation of minority voices in the dominant consensual norms that are inscribed in the cultures and practices of the public sector' (Newman, 2003: 25). As stated above, critical cultural criminology, rooted in feminist principles, could move us beyond arguments for either recognition *or* redistribution towards a common understanding of rights.

Safe spaces/dialogic spaces

Creating safe spaces for women's voices as well as residents in neighbourhoods affected by sex markets to be heard and listened to through ethnographic, participatory methods is crucial to moving debates and policy measures forward. It is also important to situate these voices within broader analyses of the state and what is possible in relation to policy reform.

Fraser argues that, currently, claims for *recognition* (identity politics) are displacing claims for *redistribution*, and that this has serious consequences:

> insofar as the politics of recognition displaces the politics of redistribution, it may actually promote economic inequality; insofar as it reifies group identities, it risks sanctioning violations of human rights and freezing the very antagonisms it purports to mediate. (Fraser, 2000: 108)

I suggest here that the current divide between feminists who view prostitution as being abuse, exploitation and violence and a further manifestation of violence against women, and feminists who support the recognition of sex worker rights to address inequalities, violence, abuse and lack of human rights is a clear example of too great a focus on claims to recognition at the expense of claims for redistribution. Redistribution is displaced by identity politics (recognition claims). We need to work across this divide and challenge sexual and social inequalities with respect to both. We also need to acknowledge that structural inequalities form the entry point for many women's routes into sex work. Poverty, the need for money, is the bottom line. Fraser argues that it is important to conceptualise

> struggles for recognition so that they can be integrated with struggles for redistribution, rather than displacing and undermining them. It also means developing an account of recognition that can accommodate the full complexity of social identities, instead of one that promotes reification and separatism. (Fraser, 2000: 109)

She goes on to suggest that instead of treating (mis)recognition through group identity (for example, sex worker = sexually exploited victim), the status of the group members should be as full and equal partners in social interaction and their status not be reduced to group identity. To be misrecognised (as victim) is to be denied the status of full partner in social interaction, 'unworthy of respect and esteem' (Fraser, 2000: 114).

In *Prostitution and feminism: Towards a politics of feeling*, I argued for a renewed methodology for social research defined as 'ethno-mimesis', incorporating visual as well as ethnographic and PAR methodologies to document the politics of everyday life for and with women selling sex, based on mutual recognition, respect and ultimately redistribution through action research. A politics of feeling describes the process of engaging with women and their lives, from their frame of reference through their inclusion in the research involving recognition, respect and participation. In the process we produce praxis as purposeful knowledge that may be transformative. The relationship between thinking, feeling and doing (Arendt, 1970; Tester, 1995), commitment and collective responsibility is central to PAR; as is the need to create the intellectual and practical spaces for women's voices to be heard, for them to participate as equal citizens, to counter 'othering' and to work towards collectively resisting and challenging sexual, social and structural inequalities.

Cultural citizenship: rights, recognition, redistribution

Some years ago now, Laclau and Mouffe (2001) wrote that radical democracy is the best route towards progressive social change (and *governance*) for the Left today. Their version of radical democracy embraces many aspects of the socialist and liberal democratic traditions. Most importantly, the ability to envision radical democracy includes the:

> circulation, radicalisation and institutionalisation of democratic discourse ... not as a set of superficial reforms, but as the struggle to institutionalise a radical pluralist imaginary. (Smith, 1998: 5)

I argue, therefore, that in producing a more holistic understanding of social justice we must transgress the boundaries of sex as work or sex as violence and acknowledge the associational, cultural and distributive aspects of justice for women towards cultural citizenship made up of rights, recognition and redistribution. In the words of Mouffe, we need to establish a 'chain of equivalence among the different democratic struggles so as to create an equivalent articulation' (Mouffe, 1995: 318) between our demands. What might the nodal points or points of intersection be? Violence and safety; sexual and social inequalities; addressing poverty; and the radical potential of feminism(s)? In previous articles (Scoular and O'Neill, 2007; O'Neill et al, 2008) I argue that establishing chains of equivalence will help to realise the counter-hegemonic role of feminism(s) through dialogue, practice and politics, but also provide the political and practical space for a renewed research agenda that uses social justice and cultural citizenship as the leverage on which to base a radical democratic approach to prostitution reform. Providing spaces for dialogue and debate is crucial.

To provide examples and visualise cultural citizenship (Pakulski, 1977), I include below three examples of art works produced by women sex workers who took part in the PAR Rosie Campbell and I conducted in Walsall, commissioned by residents of Walsall South Health Action Zone. Underpinned by the principles of PAR (inclusion, participation, valuing all voices, outcomes that are interpretive and action oriented) and working with sex workers, residents and statutory and voluntary sector agencies, we also worked with Walsall Youth Arts and Walsall Community Arts to make visible the women's (as well as residents') experiences, feelings and hopes for the future.

Redistribution

The image below (Figure 3.1) of one woman's employment history links to redistribution in that it highlights economic routes in. It makes visible economic motives for selling sex as well as challenging the viewer to think differently, to move beyond the identity of sex worker as abject 'other' and to think more holistically, in multiple ways, about the woman concerned who wants to be valued as someone who has a range of positive skills to offer employers, often gained through working in difficult circumstances.

> Your prejudices should not hinder me from progressing with my life and with my future plans to move forward.

In a recent paper Lister writes,

> One key element of a socially just distribution of income and wealth in any particular society is that all its members have sufficient material resources to live with dignity and to flourish. Despite the very welcome reductions in child and pensioner (though not working age adult) poverty achieved by New Labour, levels of poverty in Britain remain high compared with those in most of the wider European Union. (Lister, 2007: 2)

Recognition

The woman who created the next image (Figure 3.2) is asking us to think beyond the stereotypes and to recognise her for herself, not

Figure 3.1: Redistribution

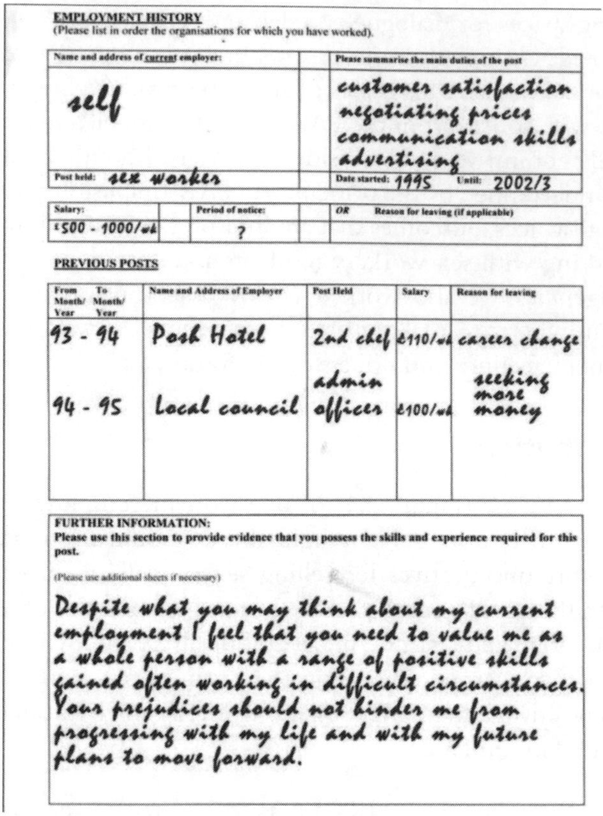

EMPLOYMENT HISTORY
(Please list in order the organisations for which you have worked).

Name and address of current employer:		Please summarise the main duties of the post
self		customer satisfaction negotiating prices communication skills advertising
Post held: sex worker		Date started: 1995 Until: 2002/3

Salary:		Period of notice:		OR Reason for leaving (if applicable)
£500 - 1000/wk		?		

PREVIOUS POSTS

From Month/Year To Month/Year	Name and Address of Employer	Post Held	Salary	Reason for leaving
93 - 94	Posh Hotel	2nd chef	£110/wk	career change
94 - 95	Local council	admin officer	£100/wk	seeking more money

FURTHER INFORMATION:
Please use this section to provide evidence that you possess the skills and experience required for this post.
(Please use additional sheets if necessary)

Despite what you may think about my current employment I feel that you need to value me as a whole person with a range of positive skills gained often working in difficult circumstances. Your prejudices should not hinder me from progressing with my life and with my future plans to move forward.

through the lens of a 'prostitute' identity. The fact that she wears a mask in the first place tells us that she has to hide her identity, so she is not recognised and labelled, stereotyped, stigmatised, made abject. Looking beyond the mask and recognising women for who and what they are, as multiple subjects, with agency, who make choices in difficult circumstances, is a central plank of any politics of inclusion with and for sex workers.

Figure 3.3 tells us that this woman is a Mother, is loved and respected by her son, is proud of the fact that her son bought her these presents. The image and words demand us to think about her in the context of her relationship with a loved son, as a loved Mother – not as a 'dirty prostitute' or any of the other abject labels and discourses used to reduce the subjecthood of women who sell sex to signifiers of disease, dirt and abjection.

Lister argues that while 'the redistribution paradigm is concerned with economic injustice; the recognition paradigm addresses cultural or symbolic injustice' (Lister, 2007: 4). Moreover, Fraser articulates this as 'nonrecognition (being rendered invisible via the authoritative

Figure 3.2: Look beyond the mask

Figure 3.3: My son bought me these rings

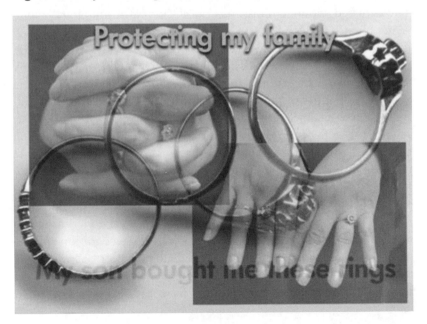

representational, communicative, and interpretative practices of one's culture) or disparaged in stereotypic public cultural representations and/or in everyday life interactions' (Fraser, 1995: 71).

Lister also writes that recognition claims are:

> All too easily dismissed as so-called 'political correctness' (particularly when recognition struggles have been expressed in terms of narrow identity politics), recognition is in fact about claims to decency and dignity. (Lister, 2007: 4)

Rights

Rights to safety from violence, rights to respect and rights to earn money are reflected in the fourth image, which also tells us very clearly that safety from violence and sexual health issues are a priority for women selling sex (Figure 3.4). Rights encompass human rights, labour rights and rights of citizenship. Discussions about human rights involve us in discussions of power and inequalities. As Lister writes, 'the costs of social *in*justice are borne, by and large, by those who lack voice and power. The struggle *for* social justice should involve us all' (Lister, 2007: 10–11). Rights, recognition and redistribution are interconnected.

Towards a coordinated prostitution strategy?

Thus, situated within feminist and critical/cultural criminology (which values phenomenological research as well as action research utilising PAR methodologies), I propose that we engage with the theories and practices of governance; think beyond the labels and binaries; and seek transformative change through dialogue and by imagining a radical democratic politics of prostitution reform *with* the very women who are the current subject-objects of reform.

Currently a focus on demand and criminalising the client is being taken up by the Home Office as a potential way forward, alongside responsibilising women to exit through rehabilitation – despite the plethora of arguments and evidence against this approach. Turning the tables on the clients will not help us to challenge the simplistic representation of the prostitute as 'other', as abject, as a victim, and so will put a further barrier in the way of promoting recognition and the inclusion of sex workers in debates and dialogues. Nor will it support processes of redistribution; instead, it provides an example of identity thinking[4] and deflects attention away from the real issues – which

Figure 3.4: Tips of the trade

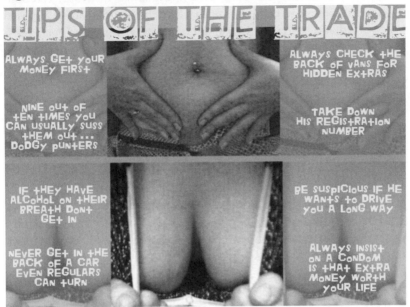

include structural and sexual inequalities within the context of global capitalism, consumerism and processes of detraditionalisation.

As I argued earlier, we do need to engage in a process of recognition through inclusion of sex workers in research, debates and dialogue, but we also need to address the issue of redistribution, poverty and economic routes in. I will close with some suggestions for further discussion and debate that may point us in the direction of an effective strategy that bears reference to the wealth of data on routes into sex work within the context of governance, Fraser's politics of recognition and redistribution, and the complex lived relations and structural/social inequalities experienced by women selling sex.

In a recent article (O'Neill et al, 2008) a team funded by the Joseph Rowntree Foundation to examine *Living and working in areas of street sex work: From conflict to co-existence* (Pitcher et al, 2006) argued that it is possible to work with local residents and community groups, sex workers and sex-work projects to develop an ongoing dialogue that takes into account the interests of different members of local communities, including sex workers (*and clients*), and ensures that the needs of sex workers are reflected in community responses to national and local policy initiatives and that helps to challenge dominant discourses and hopefully feeds into public policy at local, regional and national levels. A politics of inclusion, underpinned by what I call a politics of feeling informed by PAR methodologies and building upon

Fraser's work on the politics of recognition and redistribution, could help to foster a more nuanced approach to the realities of street-based sex work that acknowledges the dynamics of governance *and* fosters a more equitable approach to strategies for prostitution reform in the 21st century, and thus builds on strong national work in this area by feminists, practitioners and projects working to support women, men and young people.

Given the current strategy, the travesty is that an already multiply-disadvantaged group will be further disadvantaged, and a new group of disadvantaged and criminalised men will simply swell the statistics, experience stigma and ultimately add yet another layer of complexity to a chaotic system constituted by disciplinary power and the social control of 'deviant' acts, masquerading as harm minimisation and justice. This, I feel, is too high a price to pay for the semblance of community safety outlined in the strategy and needs to be addressed urgently, before the impact is felt by the projects. For it is the much-needed support to women, men and young people selling sex that should be the projects' first port of call. Prioritising exit strategies and criminalising clients will impact negatively on projects that may need to adapt in the new climate in order to gain funding, thus potentially losing some of the much-needed support services. Ultimately, at grassroots level this will impact negatively on the very women selling sex who are marginalised, stigmatised, 'othered', and mis-recognised.

Notes

[1] Borrowing from Karl Marx: 'Men make their own history, but they do not make it as they please; they do not make it under self-selected circumstances, but under circumstances existing already, given and transmitted from the past. The tradition of all dead generations weighs like an Alp on the brains of the living' (*The Eighteenth Brumaire of Louis Napoleon* (1852), available at www. marxists.org/archive/marx/works/subject/hist-mat/18-brum/ch01.htm, accessed 25 May 2008).

[2] Not the partial form of justice defined in the Home Office strategy, which is simply defined as ensuring the law is enforced.

[3] The forum was reconfigured in the mid 1990s under the combined leadership of social services and the police.

[4] Identity thinking is the way unlike things are made to appear as like (the way sectional interests are promoted as universal) and are reified or reinforced by structures, processes and practices. Clients are to be made pariahs under

the latest 'solution' to prostitution – taking the place that women sex workers have occupied for centuries.

FOUR

UK sex work policy: eyes wide shut to voluntary and indoor sex work

Teela Sanders

Introduction

The last decade has seen a proliferation of activities from central and local government, community safety partnerships and individual police forces, as well as the collective umbrella of the Association of Chief Police Officers, introducing policy and guidelines in addition to enhancing existing and new legislation in order to manage parts of the sex industry. This has been a reaction to the Home Office's review of prostitution laws and management strategies that resulted in the blueprint *A Coordinated Prostitution Strategy* (Home Office, 2006), which takes a non-tolerant approach to the sex industry, opting for 'eradication' of street prostitution and 'tackling demand' as the key focus.

This edited collection examines some of the complex and specific areas that make up what is commonly known as prostitution in the UK. To add to this analysis, this chapter examines the impact of government policy from 2004 on the female indoor sex markets and men who buy sex from women. In this chapter, 'indoor sex markets' refers to massage parlours, illegal brothels, women who work as escorts independently through the internet or agencies, or those who work alone or in small numbers from 'working flats'. I will focus on the sale of direct sexual services rather than indirect sexual services such as lap dancing, telephone sex work and stripping (see Harcourt and Donovan, 2005 for types of sex markets). The chapter has three main objectives. First, to examine the government's position on indoor sex work in contrast to street prostitution. Second, to question why the government refuses to acknowledge, debate or make provisions for voluntary sex work beyond the criminalisation agenda. Third, to explore the reasons for 'tackling demand', the mechanisms for doing so, and to discuss critically the impact and realities of making it illegal to buy sex. To achieve these objectives, the chapter reviews the two main government documents: the consultation *Paying the Price* (Home Office, 2004) and the resultant *A Coordinated Prostitution Strategy* (Home Office, 2006).

Before recent policy changes are examined it is worth briefly exploring what is meant by the nature and extent of the indoor sex markets. The laws on the indoor markets remain confused. It is not (yet) illegal to sell or buy sex between two consenting adults in the UK, and an individual can sell sex legitimately from her own home where there is no one else working, managing, assisting, living off the profits or renting out premises. The laws are concentrated around the relationships and activities that facilitate the selling of sex: procuring, soliciting and loitering, advertising and brothel keeping are all against the law (for details on the law see Brooks-Gordon, 2006). More recently, men who 'kerb crawl' on the street have been brought into the criminal justice system (this will be discussed below). Despite a proliferation of laws that make it very difficult for sex work to take place legally in the UK, arrests remain low and the industry thrives, adapts and continues to operate.

Although it is incredibly difficult to make any accurate assessment of the prevalence of the industry, there are some indications of the extent of different indoor markets. A popular UK-based website, Punternet, that matches female sex workers (usually independent escorts who are legal) with male customers, boasts that since 1999 men have posted 76,886 'field reports' (accounts of commercial sexual encounters). These reports represent a total expenditure of £9,945,353 (an average of £130 per visit).[1] Given that this website is a snapshot of the independent escort industry and it is likely that most customers in the UK do not post accounts, it can be suggested from these statistics that the independent escort market is a considerable size in terms of the numbers of female sex workers, male customers who buy sex and the flow of cash in this informal economy. Other markets that operate indoors and are usually illegal appear to be on similar scales. Moffatt and Peters (2004) estimate that in 1999, in the private parlours in the UK (illegal brothels), turnover was approximately £534 million (equivalent to cinema expenditure). It is these hidden sex markets that form the 'tip of the iceberg' in terms of the informal shadow sex economies.

Paying the Price: the invisibility of the indoor sex markets

The *Paying the Price* document has been criticised by several academics who work in different disciplines, which, taken together, suggests that the literature review that 'informed' the consultation was poorly conducted, resulting in a lack of complexity or reality, and misinformation (Soothill and Sanders, 2004; Cusick and Berney, 2005; Brooks-Gordon, 2006: 47–9). Soothill and Sanders (2004) argue that the consultation document lacks any acknowledgement of the historical legacy and legal framework in which prostitution in the UK exists. This is particularly important because the Wolfenden Committee Report (1957) specifically left a loophole in the law to enable indoor sex work to continue and did not make an attempt to criminalise the selling and buying of sexual services between consenting adults. As has been noted elsewhere, the Wolfenden Committee was careful to base its framework on the presumption that while the law should and could play an appropriate role in protecting vulnerable individuals, it was inappropriate for the law to legislate on matters of private morality. As Whowell and Gaffney show later in this volume, undermining this fundamental precept can have a devastating impact on particular sections of the community. It is the legacy of the Wolfenden Report and the framework of laws that arose from it that has enabled sex workers, who operate in their own premises, to work legally. Other criticisms have been waged against the consultation document for promoting stereotypes and misinformation about sexual health risks and sex workers. Cusick and Berney (2005) state that *Paying the Price* displays a poor understanding of sexual health risks, links health promotion to policing strategies and prioritises not sex workers' safety, but rather, the needs of the community.

Paying the Price pays scant attention to the complexities of the sex markets and the diversity of indoor markets. Only in the final chapter, 'Considering the Options', do the indoor markets appear, where the main focus of concern is those experiencing 'serious exploitation' such as 'children abused through prostitution' and 'trafficked women kept in bondage' that happens in off-street premises (Home Office, 2004: 84). These extreme sexual exploitation cases are given the bulk of the attention in the consultation paper when considering indoor markets. Although an important public protection issue which deserves high priority and resources, this attention outweighs the reality that the majority of indoor establishments are not involved in extreme exploitation or organised crime. The document does not acknowledge the other varied markets where women work independently, or the significant impact that internet technology and communication facilities such as the mobile phone have had on the organisation of the indoor markets. The growth of advertising on the internet from individual sex workers organising their business online to take 'outcalls' to hotels and houses or 'incalls' to 'working flats' has changed the shape of the market. Neither these changes nor the diversity of the sex industries are understood in the review of the sex markets.

Some international examples of licensing schemes in Victoria and New South Wales (Australia), as well as the Austrian model of registration, are put forward as options. However, again the literature drawn upon is only partial: the limitations of these models are explored, rather than the benefits. Equally, the successful models of licensing that are to be found in Nevada, Las Vegas and Germany are not included in the review. The overwhelming question that *Paying the Price* asks when considering management solutions for the indoor markets are: 'Is it ever acceptable for sex to be sold from private premises? If so, what safeguards should be put in place?' and 'Would registration help safeguard public health?' (Home Office, 2004: 88). These questions focus on the morality of selling and buying sex rather than on exploring the reality of consensual adult commercial sex. At no point in the discussion of the options for managing indoor markets is the safety of sex workers placed at the forefront of the objectives. Further, as Kinnell (2006) notes, discussion is not encouraged about the legitimacy of two adults making an arrangement to exchange sexual services for a fee. It is never questioned why this relationship is different from similar exchanges which take place in conventional relationships and settings but through less 'up-front' and obvious economic exchanges.

These misgivings can be traced back to the definition of prostitution that the Home Office adopts in the consultation and later in *A Coordinated Prostitution Strategy*. Cusick and Berney (2005: 597) point out that *Paying the Price* 'conflates sex work with wider structural problems' such as teenage pregnancy, drug use, trafficking, 'slavery' and child abuse and fails to 'disentangle abuse from sex work'. Returning to the primary definition of 'prostitution' (Home Office, 2004: 14), there is no acknowledgement of 'sex work' or that adults can voluntarily consent to selling and buying commercial sex. Later the consultation document goes on to stress that 'we need to be as clear as possible about the nature and scope of prostitution to ensure that policies and practices are based on evidence rather than myth' (Home Office, 2004: 14). Yet, from the outset there is no acknowledgement of the complex spectrum between force, exploitation and voluntary consent, or indeed the theoretical underpinnings of the arguments about exploitation or work (see Weizter, 2005). To a large extent, the policy review was set up without any real acknowledgement of the theoretical underpinnings that shape the debates about prostitution and sex work, leaving the construction of the 'problem' informed by only one side of the debate and ignoring the backdrop of feminist organising around the premise that sexual services both can be sold as labour and should be treated through the framework of employment. The government's standpoint and objectives to 'eradicate street prostitution' and to 'disrupt the sex market' are shaped by the assumption that all prostitution is damaging, unwanted and violence against women.

A Coordinated Prostitution Strategy: irresponsible policy?

This section reviews three aspects of the strategy that affect the safety of sex workers and the management of indoor premises: 'disrupting the sex markets'; why licensing indoor premises was rejected; and proposals to change the law on women working together.

Disrupting the sex markets

The strategy focuses largely on street prostitution, but the overall message of 'disrupting the sex markets' is equally applied to indoor markets. With the objectives of reducing sexual exploitation, improving the safety and quality of life for communities affected by prostitution, as well as 'tackling demand', the strategy makes no compensation for voluntary consensual sexual transactions. There were glimmers of hope that the decision makers had recognised the diversity of indoor markets and the markedly different culture and organisational properties as compared with street prostitution. However, the strategy does not accept the wider reality that there are well-managed parlours and managers who are concerned with the well-being and safety of sex workers. The reality that many brothels are operated under similar working conditions and styles of management as legitimate businesses is rejected, despite reports from those who contributed to the consultation that 'brothels should be allowed to operate as ordinary businesses' (Home Office, 2006: 60), which would allow for public health education and positive outcomes for outreach projects.

There appeared to be limited consultation with those who manage, own or work in indoor premises on what constitutes 'good' and 'bad' management, as well as a rejection that many establishments are not exploitative. Opportunities for consultation with groups who promote safe indoor sex work were available. At the time of the consultation the Manchester Sauna Owners Forum was in operation. This group, initially facilitated by the police and health workers, was made up of sauna owners who came together to set up good practice guidelines and safety regulations as well as to deal with current issues affecting their businesses. There is no evidence that this group of responsible managers was consulted. Instead, anecdotal evidence from outreach projects across the country reports that policing strategies that aim to 'disrupt the sex markets' have also been applied to indoor premises where there have been no concerns raised of exploitation or mistreatment. Parlours have been raided and closed down by licensing authorities, and managers have been arrested for brothel-keeping offences. Arresting the managers of well-organised establishments is highly counterproductive on several levels. It provides no incentives for managers to run respectable, discreet and orderly venues, or indeed to take care of the workers through fair pricing policies and good working conditions. It provides no incentive to maintain the establishment's facilities or presentation, nor any reason to seek legitimacy through paying tax, for instance. Rather than acting as a deterrent for other owners of establishments, it sends the message that an unregulated market that is sporadically policed can therefore exploit sex workers and customers without any official agencies taking note.

There also appeared to be no realisation of the impact of 'disrupting the sex markets' on individual sex workers. Like the negative impact on sex workers caused by heavy policing on the street (Sanders, 2004), policing indoor establishments that are not involved in exploitation will have the effect of reducing compliance, with women and managers not reporting crimes or engaging with the police as 'informers', weakening working relationships with harm-reduction projects and driving the industry further underground (see Boynton and Cusick, 2006). Indoor premises, while not at risk of the same dangers or levels of vulnerability as women on the street, are also at risk of crimes such as robbery and non-payment, as well as other types of violence (Sanders and Campbell, 2007). Given that there are several aspects of the indoor markets that need management and regulation in order to protect sex workers and legitimate an industry in order to stamp out (rather than encourage) exploitation, the question remains why the strategy did not attempt to regulate the brothel industry.

Why was licensing brothels rejected?

Given that the consultation document paid some attention to reviewing a selective set of international examples of licensing brothels and registration schemes, it is deeply disappointing that the final strategy did not follow up these proposed solutions. In the 'findings' of the consultation process it was reported that the 'majority' expressed scepticism about regulation, while only a 'minority' suggested licensing would be acceptable.

The 'minority' of voices who agreed with a licensing proposal is described as including men who buy sex – a group that has been described as 'users' and criminals by the strategy. As described above, those groups such as managers and owners who would perhaps agree with a licensing system were not directly consulted. There is also no evidence that the views of women who voluntarily work as sex workers in the indoor premises were consulted about their views on licensing or other solutions of management. Indeed, the merits of a licensing system are not fully explored. How a system could work in a British context was not proposed as a point for consultation, and neither was evidence of 'good' or 'professional' establishments proposed as a standard model for a new system of monitoring or checking premises. There is no evidence that other government departments were consulted, such as Customs and Excise or the Inland Revenue, or even the Department for Work and Pensions.

In the strategy, two reasons are offered for rejecting a licensing system. The first was that if such a licensing system were introduced, a hierarchical structure would develop, pushing those unwilling to comply with regulations into an illegal sector. On this point, it has already been established that there is a hierarchy of types of premises based on their professionalism and good practices (Sanders, 2005). Campbell and Farley (2006: 57) note that most sex workers distinguished between 'reasonable' and 'unreasonable' or 'good' and 'bad' management. Sex workers have operationalised the criteria that could form a set of standards that establishments must commit to as part of the licensing process. Those that did not comply could then be investigated for sexual exploitation by the appropriate agencies and the law could be used to prosecute those managers and owners who were mistreating and exploiting individuals. Given that there are tiers of brothel types, based on their working conditions, formalising a system where brothels could become legitimate would allow the authorities more control over the current system. In addition, a system of licensing would then allow policing resources to be targeted at those unregistered premises.

The second reason for rejecting a licensing system rests on the fear that any legitimate system would see an increase in the acceptance of prostitution and the expansion of the industry. On this point, although it is difficult to be conclusive, the rise of the internet and the mobile phone has already dramatically changed the shape, nature and size of the indoor sex markets, and a licensing system would not encourage more growth, but rather have the effect of ordering and managing what exists. Equally, other aspects of the sex industry, such as lap-dancing bars, strip and sex clubs are a regular and accepted part of the night-time economy and leisure industry which are licensed by local councils. The wider sexualised culture that infiltrates our everyday worlds, from magazines, advertisements, TV content and entertainment pursuits, has a significant bearing on the parameters of sexual acceptability, attitudes and availability (Attwood, 2006). In this sense, 'embourgeoisement' of the sex industry becomes part of a cultural message that legitimates sexual services of both the direct and non-direct kind (see Sanders, 2008a). A licensing system would regulate the industry as it exists and not necessarily increase the number of businesses.

The rejection of any licensing system is based on 'the aim of the Strategy to minimise the opportunities for exploitation'. It could be argued, as countries and states that have introduced licensing have, that the only way to ensure that sexual exploitation in the indoor markets is stamped out is through a regulatory system that checks the management, premises and working conditions. For instance, Laskowski (2002) explains how the German Prostitution Law (2002) set out clear guidelines for brothel management that enabled sex workers' labour rights and set up legislation that prevented sexual exploitation. Also, referring to the strictly regulated Nevada brothel system, Brents and Hausbeck identify how 'the legalisation of prostitution brings a level of public scrutiny, official regulation and bureaucratization to brothels that decreases violence' (Brents and Hausbeck, 2005: 270), affording safety and legitimacy to sex workers and preventing exploitative management. It is this side of the argument that is not considered. Instead, what Agustin (2007) terms 'the rescue industry' holds significant power over the thinking of decision makers to use broader issues of female migration and exploitation as an argument for 'disrupting' rather than managing the sex markets.

Proposal to reform the law on the definition of a brothel

The 2006 strategy does concede that the current law that prevents women working together is contrary to safety advice and proposes to alter this so that 'two (or three) individuals may work together' (Home Office, 2006: 61). This proposed change brings the law up to date with current practices, as many women who work from flats do so in small groups both for safety and to share the costs. This proposal would allow women to work without the fear of arrest for procurement or brothel keeping and would be one step towards legitimating the small-scale indoor markets. However, this proposal does not address the issue of working conditions, regulation, labour rights or financial stability for those who work indoors. Equally, there is no timetable for when this proposal will be taken forward, given parliamentary time or when the law will change. This has left many sex workers unclear about where the law stands, what is legitimate and what is not. Simply, there is no action plan relating to this recommendation, and at the time of writing there is little evidence that there will be any changes to the laws on brothel keeping or any clearer direction from the Home Office on the place of voluntary sex work in policy.

The focus on 'demand'

Over the last decade, men who buy sex have been increasingly criminalised. The 1985 Sexual Offences Act marked the first piece of legislation to include the offence of kerb crawling and introduced two offences. First, that of 'kerb-crawling' as soliciting another person from a 'motor vehicle' or 'in a street or public place' that is 'likely to cause annoyance to the person ... or nuisance to the other persons in the neighbourhood' (1985 Sexual Offences Act, section 1). The second offence is that of 'persistent soliciting' of a man who solicits another person in a public place for the services of a prostitute (1985 Sexual Offences Act, section 2). This offence only carried the severity of a level 3 fine (approximately £400) and was not arrestable but arranged through a letter ordering the accused to attend the magistrates' court. Legislation has continued to increase the powers of arrest against men for kerb crawling and finally, under the 2001 Criminal Justice and Police Act, kerb crawling was made an arrestable offence.

In the *Paying the Price* consultation document it was immediately clear that the government's standpoint on men who purchased sex was that they were perpetrators. As Whowell and Gaffney in this volume suggest, *Paying the Price* vilifies men in the sex industry. The language of the document firmly states the position of the government: men who buy sex are referred to as 'the user' (Home Office, 2004: 16). The position of men who buy sex was immediately equated with exploitation, danger, violence and generally an activity that should not be tolerated, debated or accepted in modern society. In the document, men who buy commercial sex are conflated with those who perpetuate criminal activities, evident in the statement: 'going to a prostitute can mean supporting the illegal drugs industry' (Home Office, 2004: 12). These same views were promoted on the Home Office website in 2007, justifying the campaign against kerb crawlers because they 'indirectly support drug dealers and abusers whilst perpetuating a market fraught with violence and abuse'.[2] However, this perspective on men who buy sex was vastly at odds with Home Office research that suggests the 'user' is a 30-year-old male who is married, in full-time employment and has no criminal record (Hester and Westmarland, 2004: 143).

The consultation document was criticised by researchers and academics, who highlighted the gross lack of evidence gathered from the existing body of research about men who buy sex. Brooks-Gordon (2005) argued that minimal research and evidence had been collated and applied to the review, and that there was generally a negative and unfair view of men who buy sex. Phoenix and Oerton (2005: 77) note that, by the end of the consultation process, prostitution had been reframed as a 'social problem' and that this had been achieved by crafting and promoting a specific attitude towards men who buy sex, such that they became part of a wider 'problem of men' discourse, evident in New Labour's social and criminal justice policies (see Scourfield and Drakeford, 2002).

In *A Coordinated Prostitution Strategy* there is a two-pronged approach to managing prostitution. First, that of eradicating street prostitution (see Scoular et al, O'Neill and Melrose in this volume). The second is a staggered approach to enforcing the law on 'kerb crawling' leading to prosecution: informal warning letters to men spotted in 'red light areas'; court diversion through kerb crawler re-education programmes; prosecution using existing financial penalties, including disqualification from driving; and 'naming and shaming' tactics through the local media.

The current political debate is one in which criminalising men is considered the most effective way to reduce sexual exploitation. At the time of writing the Home Office is undertaking another review, entitled 'Tackling Demand', which involves examining different systems that criminalise the purchaser of sex. Media hype and deterrent warning campaigns (see Morgan Thomas, Chapter Eight, this volume), strong moral messages from voluntary groups and a call from a small group of female MPs for making the purchase of sex a crime has been controlling the direction of policy.[3] The explicit hatred for 'men who buy', which also shows a profound misunderstanding of the nature of the relationships between some sex workers and their clients (see Sanders, 2008b), is repeatedly aired by certain MPs in parliamentary debates. For example, Denis MacShane, MP for Rotherham, stated: 'Frankly, too many dirty old, middle-aged and young men think that by putting down a few pounds they can abuse women, often under the age of 18, who are trafficked into our country and appear in adverts such as the ones in the local papers' (*Hansard*, 27 November 2007, col 8). The continued imagery of men who buy sex as 'dirty', 'diseased' and 'uncivil' is coupled with the discourse of the tragic victim of trafficking that is at the forefront of all prostitution policy.

Why criminalising men is flawed

Arguments have been put forward which explain clearly why it is a flawed policy to address the sex industry by criminalising men who pay for sex. O'Connell Davidson (2003) draws on empirical findings from a multi-site pilot study across six countries throughout the world (O'Connell Davidson, 2003) to oppose the arguments for penalising men who buy sex as the solution to effectively reducing the abuse of women. First, there are significant cross-cultural differences in the social meanings of the consumption of sex. There are complex differences in the pressure to perform masculinity by either engaging in commercial sex or abstaining from it, at various life stages and ages, meaning that 'normal' masculinity is closely linked with the sex industry. Second, young men and boys are more likely to come under social pressures to engage with the sex industry, suggesting that cultural norms dictate who is buying sex. For instance, it is an acceptable social ritual in the UK for young men to engage in alcohol-fuelled events which include taking part in the sex industry around milestones such as 18th and 21st birthdays and stag parties. Third, how clients perceive migrant sex workers is not simply an expression of mastery over a female body but involves racial or ethnic hierarchies and 'a complex configuration of attitudes towards race, migration, sexuality and prostitution' (O'Connell Davidson, 2003: 56).

Finally, O'Connell Davidson documents and argues against the abolitionist call to penalise men who buy sex because clients display abhorrence towards forced prostitution and trafficking and are concerned with engaging in only 'free' prostitution. My own research with men who buy sex from indoor sex workers confirms that many men are very aware of the issues relating to the forced, coerced or trafficked conditions under which some women work (see Sanders, 2008a, chapter 3). As a result, the men I interviewed had their own rules of engagement, in terms of which establishments they approached and which 'types' of women they purchased services from. For instance, there was a strong feeling among the men that women should be working by their own 'choice' and have autonomy over their work and conditions. Methods of avoiding contact with women who may have been coerced were to visit women who displayed a high degree of control over their businesses, which could be identified via their website marketing, and also not visiting women from Eastern Europe, which was considered a trigger in identifying coercion.

Such evidence clearly identifies the homogeneity of men who buy sex, and how a 'one size fits all' approach that places men at the centre of any legislative system is a flawed, naive policy response. Among men who buy sex there are strong opinions about the importance of consent and voluntary engagement in sex work. It is a myth that 'demand' refers to the majority of clients who are abusive, or who take pleasure in seeking out women who are coerced and selling sex against their consent (see Sanders and Campbell, 2008).

There is also no evidence from other countries where it has been made a crime to buy sex that such an approach is successful. The Swedish system that criminalised paying for sexual service in 1998 (Ekberg, 2004) is heralded by the government as an approach that should be taken seriously and potentially imported to the UK. However, apart from an immediate decrease in street prostitution in Stockholm, the sex industry has only been displaced to indoor markets and other areas, including other countries nearby. It is certainly the case that where there is a heavy policing effort on men who buy sex, female sex workers are placed in more danger and have very limited access to harm-reduction and sexual health services (see Phoenix, Chapter One, this volume).

The dangers to sex workers that are the consequences of criminalising men can be illustrated in several ways. First, 'good customers' who do not have violent, criminal or even unfair intentions such as bartering the price, are removed from the street market because they are warned off by the high-profile policing and the criminal consequences of their actions. This deterrence exists where it is illegal to buy sex or, as in the UK, where sporadic kerb-crawler operations take place. Hence, 'bad customers' who target sex workers as vulnerable victims for robbery, violence, coercion and extreme abuse such as murder are those that are not put off by the law but instead continue to target sex workers. Taking away consenting and responsible clients from sex workers has the potential of leaving those men with abusive intentions as the core customer base. In this regard, sex workers' safety is ignored while sending out the 'correct' (sexual) moral message to the public is maintained.

Second, under conditions of criminality, sex workers will change their safer working practices and habits and work more dangerously. Sanders (2004) identifies the risks that sex workers take when they are trying to avoid the police: working later into the night; working alone; avoiding support services; taking less time to screen their clients (Sanders, 2005); accepting low prices and potentially unsafe sex because of the limited numbers of clients; taking on more strangers rather than repeat customers, who are safer and less likely to commit offences.

Third, the effects of displacement are significant in terms of further marginalising street sex workers, who are already excluded from mainstream services. It has already been demonstrated that street sex workers are further marginalised from important health services (Jeal and Salisbury, 2004; 2007). Pitcher (2006) identifies the vital support services that are often a primary source of care for women who are excluded from accessing mainstream services. Policing that causes displacement means that it is much harder for projects to find women and deliver an effective, consistent service. Policing, from the law enforcement agencies as well as resident community groups, becomes a barrier to providing sexual health, safety, drug treatment, arrest referral and other vital services. This is because sex workers become even less visible as they find alternative ways to work and become less trusting of official agencies. More recently, where projects are expected to form partnership working relationships with the police and other statutory agencies that work from a criminal and eradication agenda, relationships between sex workers and voluntary projects are tested as issues of confidentiality and trust become compromised by the demands from policing agencies. While there is evidence of clear benefits of partnership work between the police and outreach projects concerning the safety for sex workers, such as with the Ugly Mug schemes (Penfold et al, 2004), there are other instances where women are put in danger because of the eradication agenda.

Fourth, another strong reason why 'tackling demand' will not address any issues relating to the existence of conditions under which women sell sex is that the root causes of why women enter the sex industry and how they experience the industry are not addressed. Take the simple assertion made by the Labour MP Harriet Harman, that by criminalising men who buy sex there will be a direct effect on international trafficking.[4] Such an assertion fails on several levels. First, there is already a plethora of laws, many under the 2003 Sexual Offences Act, that provide adequate and tough powers to convict those who traffic people for the purposes of sexual exploitation and have sex with those under the age of 18. More important, there is a lack of understanding of the extent of trafficked women into the sex industry in the UK, which stems largely from a simple equation that all migrant sex workers are trafficked. Agustin (2006) highlights the complex push and pull factors that contribute to why women leave their home nations to migrate to other countries where they consent to work in the sex industry, or other industries such as domestic, agriculture or care work. These push and pull factors are rooted in global inequalities rather than in the single factor that there is a demand to buy sexual services.

Conclusion

There are some significant implications if there is inaction regarding the legality of indoor sex work. First, *A Coordinated Prostitution Strategy* highlights that crimes against sex workers should be considered as crimes and that violence should be taken seriously in an endeavour to 'ensure justice'. Not allowing women to work together indoors directly opposes this by increasing the dangers for an already vulnerable group of women. Evidence from several countries, including comparative studies across cities in the UK, demonstrates that the indoor sex markets where women can work together are safer than other markets (see Sanders and Campbell, 2007). Working indoors provides an inherently safer environment and affords women the chance to take crime prevention strategies seriously.

Second, increasing criminalisation of sex workers and sex work environments discourages 'good practice' in brothels and allows exploitation and coercion where none originally existed. Where there are examples of good practice relating to working conditions and the treatment of sex workers, brothel owners are given no incentive to continue or improve this. Examples of good practice gain no cultural weight within localities and, with no route for legitimating their businesses or for gaining official recognition, brothel owners are left to use exploitative practices relating to conditions, rules of engagement with clients, prices paid by sex workers to work in the establishment and so forth.

Third, policy is increasingly concerned with 'human trafficking' in the sex industry, despite low levels of official data, and with that, the once-tolerated indoor markets are increasingly targeted by policing operations. Operation Pentameter was launched in February 2006 and heralded as the first-ever national campaign against trafficking for sexual exploitation. The key objectives of Pentameter were to recover victims, and in the first wave of the operation only 84 'trafficked' women were 'recovered'. There are concerns that anti-trafficking measures are not appropriately separated from immigration service actions, with implications for trafficked and non-trafficked migrant women. As the 'rescue industry' gains increasing force to 'recover' and 'save' women from exploitative situations, the lines between migrant women voluntarily involved in the sex industry and the 'trafficked' victim become blurry in policy and policing practice (Agustin, 2007). This has the ill effect of simply policing non-nationals, with no right to remain or special process to provide protection for those women who are 'rescued'. The general practice of deporting 'victims' suggests that trafficking policy is a shoddy disguise for policing migrant women.

Fourth, police raids on brothels and premises where there is no direct intelligence that 'trafficking' is taking place have been reported to advocacy organisations. Long-standing brothels have been closed down and managers who have provided good working conditions and terms of employment for sex workers have been reported, to be charged with brothel-keeping offences. Closing down brothels where exploitation is not apparent is detrimental, as it diverts policing and legal resources away from the premises that are exploitative and infringe individual women's labour rights. Closing down premises that are reputable reduces the available options for sex workers, removes the 'good' employers and leaves space for underground businesses and organised crime to emerge and grow.

If New Labour continues to refuse to provide a legitimate system whereby indoor premises can be legalised and regulated to agreed standards and women can be protected, the underworld of the sex industry will only grow. The reason it will not be eradicated, despite efforts to 'disrupt the markets', is that the sex market is built upon strong forces of *both* supply *and* demand. Bernstein (2001; 2007) notes that the 'unbridled ethic of consumption' of contemporary society extends to sexual commodification as a viable and accepted aspect of late capitalism, while at the same time the middle classes are taking refuge in the sex industry as both buyers and sellers of sex. The supply side of the sex industry is buoyant, as middle-class nationals enter the sex markets while the 'push factors' continue to fuel the flow of female migration from the developing southern world to the affluent West. The informal economy of the sex markets is an increasingly attractive job for groups of men and women such as students (Roberts et al, 2007) and migrants who often expect that the sex industry will be part of their wider transition to a new economy and society as someone without rights and citizenship. Until UK policy takes seriously the permanence and proliferation of the sex industry and addresses the sex industry as an informal economy, the indoor markets will remain tainted with exploitation by the state, profiteers and irresponsible clients.

Notes

[1] These statistics were taken from Punternet, www.punternet.com/frs/fr_stats. php, 19 December 2007.

[2] Campaign to deter kerb crawling: www.homeoffice.gov.uk/documents/kerb-crawling-marketing-material

[3] 'UK should outlaw paying for sex', http://news.bbc.co.uk/1/hi/uk_politics/7153358.stm

[4] http://news.bbc.co.uk/1/hi/uk_politics/7153358.stm, 20 December 2007.

FIVE

Out on the streets and out of control? Drug-using sex workers and the prostitution strategy

Margaret Melrose

Addiction to drugs, too often acquired with tragic carelessness, may take control of a life, and force actions not dreamed of before. (From the film *Drug Addiction, USA*, 1951, cited in Campbell, 2000: 149)

This chapter critically considers the assumptions underlying policy proposals for sex-working drug users and drug-using sex workers in New Labour's prostitution strategy. In critiquing these underlying assumptions this discussion suggests that the strategy proposed in *A Coordinated Prostitution Strategy* (Home Office, 2006) (hereafter referred to as 'the strategy') reduces involvement in street sex work to a problem of drug use (Melrose, 2007) and at the same time misconceives problems of drug addiction. I argue that the punitive framework that has increasingly characterised policy towards problem drug users (Buchanan, 2004) has been imported into 'the prostitution debate' and now also frames policy responses to street sex workers (Scoular et al, 2007). Its potential to tackle the very real social problems experienced by those involved in street sex work is therefore severely compromised.

The chapter argues that by conflating sex work with other social problems, particularly drug addiction (see, for example, Cusick and Berney, 2005; Melrose, 2006a), the strategy conveniently sidesteps the wider structural problems associated with involvement in street sex work, such as poverty, social exclusion and homelessness. This means that what the strategy offers is punitive responses that provide 'individualised solutions to de-contextualised social problems' (Phoenix, 2003), rather than structural solutions to socially contextualised social problems (Buchanan, 2004; Cusick and Berney, 2005; Melrose, 2006a).

Sex-working drug users and drug-using sex workers

Previously, I have argued that it is conceptually important to distinguish between 'sex-working drug users' and 'drug-using sex workers' (Melrose, 2007). While this distinction may appear pedantic, it is an important distinction to make for the development of appropriate policy and practice. The distinction allows us to differentiate those individuals who are involved in sex work but whose drug use is not necessarily problematic from those individuals for whom there is a closer and more problematic connection between their drug use and their involvement in sex work. So 'sex-working drug users' may be, for instance, sex workers who are also recreational drug users. In contrast, 'drug-using sex workers' may be those individuals for whom drug usage has become problematic and/or those who engage in sex work specifically to fund their drug use.

Drawing such a distinction enables us to move beyond the idea that *all* those who participate in street sex work do so because they have problems with drugs, as is implied in the strategy. Acknowledging this distinction requires us to seek alternative explanations for some people's engagement in street sex work, and therefore alternative solutions to those proposed in the strategy.

Making this distinction does not minimise the problems that sex workers who have drug problems experience. Nor does it suggest that there are not concerning links between sex and drug markets. These problems and the links and overlaps between sex and drug markets have been confirmed by previous research (May et al, 1999; 2001; Melrose et al, 1999; Hester and Westmarland, 2004). These links are not entirely surprising, however, given that sex work, drug use and drug dealing are activities located within the realms of the informal, 'shadow' or illicit economy (O'Connell-Davidson, 1998; Melrose, 2005).

This informal and illicit economy has flourished in Britain since the 1980s, as a result of economic restructuring, welfare retrenchment and increasing levels of poverty and social exclusion (Jordan and Redley, 1994; Jordan, 1996; 1999; Dean and Melrose, 1999). In particular, this economy has become securely established in those areas that have been cut off from the economic mainstream. These informal markets provide 'alternative opportunities' (Craine, 1997) for those living on the social and economic margins of society (Dean and Melrose, 1997; 1999; Seddon, 2006). While involvement in these markets might be regarded as a 'poor choice', such involvement 'has been influenced by a range of powerful negative pressures and aggravating factors that have limited the alternatives and opportunities' (Buchanan, 2004: 390) available to those living in these areas.

Markets in heroin and, more recently, crack-cocaine have grown substantially since the mid 1980s and these are increasingly the drugs of choice for street sex workers who use drugs (see, for example, Crosby and Barrett, 1997; Faugier and Sergeant, 1997; Pearce, 1997; Plant, 1997; May et al, 1999; Melrose et al, 1999; May et al, 2001; Hester and Westmarland, 2004). Nevertheless, evidence from the Home Office-funded programme 'Tackling Prostitution: What Works?' demonstrates significant regional variations in the use of crack-cocaine, use of heroin and use of both crack-cocaine and heroin by street sex workers. This programme of research found the lowest rates of crack-cocaine use among female sex workers in Hull (45%) and the highest in Kirklees (80%); lowest rates of heroin use were among women working in Manchester (74%) and highest among women working in Bournemouth (100%). The lowest rates of both heroin and crack-cocaine use were found among women in Hull (45%) and highest among women in Kirklees (76%) (Hester and Westmarland, 2004: 80).

These findings demonstrate that a significant proportion of women involved in street sex work are not necessarily involved as a result of drug use. For these women, as for many others involved in sex work, 'poverty is the bottom line' (Edwards, 1997; O'Neill, 1997; O'Connell-Davidson, 1998; Melrose et al, 1999; O'Neill, 2001; Jones and Sagar, 2001; Phoenix, 2001). For some women, in the face of poverty, prostitution comes to represent a 'gendered survival strategy', and at the level of neoclassical economics, involvement in prostitution 'makes sense' (Phoenix, 2001). It is therefore poverty, together with previous experiences of neglect and/or abuse, combined with local conditions (McLeod, 1982 cited in O'Neill, 2001), that drives many women to the streets (Matthews, 1986) and prompts the decision to allow others to exercise powers of sexual command over them (O'Connell-Davidson, 1998). And it is poverty, *sometimes but not always in conjunction with drug use*, that serves to keep them there (Melrose et al, 1999; Jones and Sagar, 2001; O'Neill, 2001; Phoenix, 2001).

Although the public consultation document issued by the government prior to the development of the strategy avoided mentioning poverty, it did acknowledge that 'debt' as well as drug addiction played 'a major part' in 'driving people into prostitution as a survival activity' (Home Office, 2004: 39). At the same time its sister publication noted the 'absolute poverty that many women and young people involved in prostitution' experienced (Hester and Westmarland, 2004: x).

Despite this evidence of 'debt' and 'absolute poverty', the Home Office appeared to decide that it was addiction to drugs such as heroin and/or crack-cocaine that represented the most significant barrier to exiting prostitution. By emphasising this barrier and ignoring those presented by poverty, homelessness, 'unemployment, pimps, fines, low levels of income support and child support systems that penalise women (including victims of domestic violence) who refuse to name the fathers of their children' (Jones and Sagar, 2001), the prostitution strategy reduces involvement in street sex work to a problem of drug use. In so doing the strategy underestimates the difficulties faced by those women who may want to leave the streets.

Because it assumes that involvement in street sex work is reducible to a problem of drug misuse the prostitution strategy suggests that street sex workers can be removed from the streets by coercing them into drug treatment regimes. In doing so, the strategy produces a policy response that is doomed to fail, because it neglects wider structural problems and does not take account of the social and economic circumstances in which people become ensnared in sex work and/or problematic drug use (Buchanan, 2004; Cusick and Berney, 2005; Neale et al, 2006; Melrose, 2006a; 2007).

Threatened communities

Within the agenda of 'community safety', street sex workers and problematic drug users have come to appear to the government as an 'aggregate problem population' (Matthews and Pitts, 2001). At the core of the prostitution strategy is not a concern with the welfare of women and young people involved in sex work, but the need to remove the politically embarrassing problem of sex workers from the streets 'like so many bags of garbage' (Melrose, 2003).

This imperative means that New Labour is seeking a quick fix, rather than long-term solutions, to the problems posed by the existence of street sex markets. This makes it convenient to reduce involvement in street sex work to a problem of drug use, and impractical to acknowledge the wider structural problems from which street sex work and problematic drug use derive. Acknowledging these wider structural problems would require politically unpopular solutions to deeply entrenched social and economic inequalities.

The desire to retain political power through delivering 'community safety' has led New Labour to develop a punitive policy agenda which has institutionalised intolerance towards various marginalised groups (Muncie, 2000). This agenda of intolerance increasingly frames policy towards street sex workers (Scoular et al, 2007) *and* problem drug users (Barton, 1999; Buchanan, 2004). It leads to the assertion in the prostitution strategy that 'street prostitution is not an activity that we can tolerate in our towns and cities' (Home Office, 2006: 1). Invoking this collective 'we' ignores contemporary empirical evidence suggesting that street sex workers are largely tolerated in and by the communities in which they work (Scoular et al, 2007) and that street sex workers often themselves live in those communities (Melrose, 2003; Pitcher et al, 2006; Scoular et al, 2007). In so doing this policy constructs street sex workers as threatening 'others' to the communities in which they live and work. A similar process has been identified in relation to problem drug users. As Buchanan writes:

> This othering of illicit drug users is reinforced and institutionalised as the Government portrays problem drug users as a menace to society, and seeks to protect 'us' from the dangers 'they' pose. (Buchanan, 2004: 394)

Othering the other

The 'othering' processes described above are not without historical precedents. Historically, the bodies, life-styles, sexual values and morals of women involved in sex work have been constructed as a threat to the social order (Phoenix, 2001) because they were said to undermine dominant sexual and social mores. As the putative bearers of sexual diseases, women involved in prostitution were also thought to pose specific health threats. Similarly, in the 19th century drug-using women were discursively constructed as 'a threat to orderly social reproduction and civilisation itself' (Campbell, 2000: 57). Drug 'addiction', often associated with women drug users, emerged early in the 20th century as 'a hybrid construct of vice, disease and crime: a catchall category for moral, mental or social inadequacy and sexual deviance' (Campbell, 2000: 71).

'Addiction', like leprosy, was believed to have a contagious quality and women were regarded as 'agents who transmitted addiction, often through prostitution' (Campbell, 2000: 152). Women were thus blamed for 'infecting' and 'corrupting' men and, in an early reversal of the 'white slave trade' theme, in 1915 the YMCA campaigned 'to persuade the authorities that prostitutes around the great railway termini were drugging soldiers and robbing them' and requested special constables to 'keep the women from molesting soldiers' (Kohn, 2001: 31).

Contemporary Home Office constructions of street sex workers and problem drug users as a generalised 'threat' to communities have meant that the Home Office now positions itself as the last bastion of defence against these 'threatening' 'others'. In its prostitution strategy, therefore, the Home Office promises to protect communities from the 'threat' that street sex workers are said to pose. To achieve this end it mobilises myths about drug addiction and bases its policy proposals for street-based sex workers on misconceptions about the relationship between sex work and drug use, constructing involvement in the former as solely a consequence of the latter.

Fictions of addiction

Various commentators have noted the punitive and moral agenda in the reforms to prostitution policy that have occurred since New Labour came to power (Cusick and Berney, 2005; Melrose, 2006a; 2007; McNaughton and Sanders, 2007). In *A Coordinated Strategy* involvement in street sex work is represented as the consequence of a 'chemical compulsion' (Carnwath and Smith, 2002: 75) – that is, it is a compulsion to take drugs that determines involvement in street sex work. This suggests that engagement in sex work is an irrational behaviour (driven by drug addiction) rather than a rational response to a given set of historical, political, social and economic circumstances.

By mobilising this representation, the prostitution strategy is able to construct drug addiction, rather than poverty, social inequality and social exclusion, as the central narrative of street sex work. This leads to the foregrounding of the suggestion that drug treatment programmes are the means by which street sex workers might exit prostitution. This fallacy not only pretends that drug addiction can be tackled in isolation from other factors that keep women involved in street sex work, but also relies on misconceptions about the nature of drug use and/or drug dependence. Such misconceptions have been described as 'pharmaco-mythology' (Szasz, 1972 cited in Carnwath and Smith, 2002: 74). That is, the prostitution strategy is based on common myths about drug use (especially heroin) and drug addiction that circulate freely in contemporary culture. As Carnwath and Smith (2002: 74) have pointed out, pharmaco-mythology is 'no basis for policy'.

These myths suggest that all heroin users become caught up in a spiral of decline once they have started using the drug and end up as chaotic 'junkies' whose behaviour is determined by their internal chemistry (addiction to drugs) rather than their own agency and rational thought processes. However, community studies have shown that people are able to use heroin for a period of time and then 'give up without ever requiring treatment' (Carnwath and Smith, 2002). Moreover, four common patterns of heroin use and types of heroin user have been identified which suggest that it is only a small proportion of heroin users who reach the 'street junkie' stage of their heroin-using careers. Thus, users are categorised as 'occasional users', 'stable users', 'freewheeling users' and 'street junkies' (Faupel, 1991, cited in Carnwath and Smith, 2002: 79). These different patterns of use crucially depend 'on two key elements: the availability of the drug and the underlying structure of the user's life' (Carnwath and Smith, 2002: 80).

Patterns of controlled or occasional heroin use have been confirmed by a number of studies (Carnwath and Smith, 2002: 81; Warburton et al, 2005; McSweeney and Turnbull, 2007) and evidence would suggest that it is possible to remain physically and mentally healthy 'even if you use heroin every day for most of your life' (Carnwath and Smith, 2002: 73). Nevertheless, it is the image of the 'street junkie' that captures media attention, public imagination and government policy initiatives, because 'as junkies, drug users suddenly become visible' (Carnwath and Smith, 2002: 85). Their visibility, however, does not make them 'typical' heroin users. The careers of typical heroin users vary over time 'with stable or controlled use being the norm interspersed with episodes of chaotic consumption and hand-to-mouth penury' (Carnwath and Smith, 2002: 85; Holden, 2006).

Chaotic drug use (that is, the 'street junkie' stage) tends to take root in the most deprived neighbourhoods and communities (SEU 2004: 11; Melrose, 2006b), where the demand for solace or escape is 'vociferous' (Pitts, 2000). The 'new' heroin users identified by Parker et al were 'basically poor, undereducated, unemployed, and marginalised' and 'living in deprived urban environments' (Parker et al, 2001: 4). In this context chaotic drug use represents 'a symptom – and a vivid symbol – of deeper dynamics of social marginalisation and alienation' (Bourgois, 1996: 2).

Nevertheless, people who use Class A drugs are diverse and varied, as are their reasons for using them. Studies have shown that the situation of female drug users 'can only be understood by locating their lives, their illicit drug use and their income generating activities within the context of a specific set of localised socio-economic and cultural developments' (Maher and Curtis, 1992: 221).

The prostitution strategy does not try to understand street sex workers' drug use within this context and actually *decontextualises* sex workers' lives, drug use and income-generating strategies from local socio-economic and cultural conditions. It treats drug-using sex workers as a homogeneous group and focuses primarily on providing drug treatment at the cost of, for example, providing stable housing and alternative income-generating opportunities. The reality for many people involved in street sex work is that they do not have alternative means of income generation outside of prostitution. The prostitution strategy, however, suggests that street sex workers should enter drug treatment so that they can exit prostitution, but given their lack of alternative opportunities for income generation, this would not represent a rational choice. The Home Office's prostitution strategy appears not to understand that 'nobody will put significant effort into change to be worse off than they are' (Harris, 2006: 75), and to expect them to do so would be completely irrational.

The strategy asserts that 'the first step towards the stabilisation of those involved in prostitution must be to set them free of drug addiction that constantly forces them back onto the street' (Home Office, 2006: 43). Experts in the field of drug addiction, however, acknowledge that there is a need to stabilise the drug user's situation *before* intervention if that intervention is to be successful (Harris, 2006). Furthermore, it has been argued that rather than drug addiction, the key determinants of women becoming 'trapped' in prostitution are 'structural, political, cultural and legal factors as well as cognitive transformations and agency' (Sanders, 2007: 74). Research has also shown that in order for women to make successful transitions out of sex work they need both material *and* ontological support and security in order to fashion new lives for themselves (McNaughton and Sanders, 2007).

By focusing on sex workers' drug use rather than their material and ontological needs and 'the social context and underlying causes of their dependence' the prostitution strategy risks 'wrongly thinking that positive and constructive lifestyle changes can be achieved once the person is drug free and has overcome their physical and psychological dependence on the drug' (Buchanan, 2004: 391). This takes little account of the difficulties involved in trying to change the self or one's life while the social structural and environmental conditions in which that self is subjectively experienced remain unchanged (Eaton, 1993; Taylor, 1993).

Compelling treatment

In the world of drug treatment and drug use, it has been noted that since the introduction of the 1998 Crime and Disorder Act there has been a shift away from health-related, welfare-based interventions and outcomes for clients with drug problems and a move towards criminal justice interventions and crime reduction outcomes (Barton, 1999; Buchanan, 2004). Previously, harm prevention and harm minimisation approaches would have provided 'needle exchanges, prescribing services, promotion of safer practices, information services, detoxification units, Hepatitis and HIV prevention measures' and so on. Criminal justice agencies, on the other hand, 'will promote coercive measures to direct, monitor and enforce treatment' (Buchanan, 2004: 389).

The criminal justice system now has a plethora of measures to bring to bear against drug-using offenders. These include: Drug Treatment and Testing Orders (DTTOs); Abstinence Orders; Acceptable Behaviour Contracts (ABCs); Anti-Social Behaviour Orders (ASBOs); Community Rehabilitation Orders (CROs); Drug Intervention Programmes (DIPs); and Criminal Justice Intervention Programmes (CJIPs) delivered through Criminal Justice Intervention Teams (CJITs), which are located within Drug Action Teams (DATs).

It has not gone unnoticed that locating drug treatment services within a criminal justice context has a tendency to 'criminalise' the discourse of social policy, as well as the potential to alienate prospective service users (Blagg et al, 1988: 206, cited in Barton, 1999: 473; Gilling and Barton, 1997: 77, cited in Barton, 1999: 474). There are particular concerns about the use of CJIP interventions, and Parker et al have suggested that an unintended consequence of these will mean that:

> Customers will construct their biographies and accounts (of their drug use) with great care, not being sure if even their key drugs worker can really be trusted. (Parker et al, 2001: 383)

As Buchanan (2004: 389) has pointed out, delivery of drug treatment services through criminal justice agencies 'raises issues concerning assessment, motivation and appropriate referral, as well as ethical issues'. Concerns have also been expressed about the partnership working and 'information sharing' required by the 1998 Crime and Disorder Act, with fears that it will actually involve a one-way flow of information from health and other service providers 'towards criminal justice needs' (Barton, 1999: 474). This has the potential to undermine the autonomy of health sector and other workers (Barton, 1999; Parker, 2004) and compromise the confidential nature of services currently offered to people who use drugs problematically. This makes it less likely that they will come forward to receive support and services.

These reservations and concerns notwithstanding, the Home Office has made similar provisions for coercing street sex workers into drug treatment services in its prostitution strategy. While the strategy proposes measures that it describes as 'tackling demand' (for street sex work), some of the proposals are about tackling the supply side of street sex work, as many of the measures target street sex workers rather than their clients. In particular, the Home Office proposes a new 'staged' approach to the policing of street sex work (that is, policing the supply side). This 'staged' approach involves four stages, three of which precede prosecution. These are:

- Stage 1: voluntary referral, where outreach services are provided to street-based sex workers which enable the women concerned to be referred to a 'range of services' and given 'long term personal support to follow a route out of prostitution' (Home Office, 2006: 38).
- Stage 2: 'pre-court diversion', where, under the auspices of the Drug Intervention Programme, women can be offered 'a route into drug treatment when an offender is engaged with a Criminal Justice Integrated Team (CJIT) in the community' (Home Office, 2006: 38). Such schemes, also known as 'arrest referral', seek 'the voluntary engagement of drug using offenders' with drug workers who are placed in custody suites in police stations. However, in the evaluation of projects providing support packages to women to exit prostitution, arrest referral schemes were shown to be of 'limited success' and 'appeared to depend on the extent to which women accepted arrest as an "occupational hazard"' (Hester and Westmarland, 2004: ix), which of course many of them do (for example, Melrose et al, 1999).
- Stage 3 is 'following charge'. Here the Home Office turns to provisions introduced in the 2005 Drugs Act which give the police additional powers to test for drugs after arrest (previously it was after charge), while retaining the power to test after charge. Those who test positive for drugs are now required 'to undergo an assessment of their drug use'. Crucially, *failure to comply with the requirement will be an offence*' (Home Office, 2006: 39, my italics).

The Home Office defends this measure on the grounds that it will enable people who commit offences in order to fund their drug use to be 'directed' into treatment earlier. Some may object to the term 'directed' here and suggest that the more appropriate term is actually 'forced', for if failure to comply with an order to undertake a drug use assessment is an offence, people will have little choice but to comply if they are to avoid a criminal conviction (Barton, 1999; Buchanan, 2004). Ensuring that street sex workers comply with drug treatment orders by threatening penal sanctions takes no account of the fact that some drug-using sex workers may not want to stop using drugs.

The strategy seems to assume that problem drug users 'should want to give up drugs' (Buchanan, 2004: 291). Currently, however, street sex workers who are in touch with dedicated projects and/or outreach services can be referred voluntarily to drug treatment services, but many do not seek such referrals. Where they do, drug treatment services do not always have the capacity to meet the demand, as in many areas drug treatment services are overstretched and demand for services outstrips supply (Barton, 1999; Malloch, 2004; Parker, 2004). Moreover, existing services have been developed to respond largely to the needs of male heroin users and they may therefore have difficulty 'in moulding women into the resources they have created' (Malloch, 2004: 300; Harding, 2006). There is a serious lack of female-only provision, especially in residential units, yet evidence suggests that women's treatment outcomes are better when treatment is provided in all-female environments, and the public consultation exercise did recommend that female-only treatment provision should be made available. Obviously, 'if these services are not in place for women the courts are likely to have little success in fast-tracking women into them' (Malloch, 2004: 303).

Besides this, if someone does not seek help for a drug problem voluntarily there is every possibility that the treatment will not succeed and the person concerned may be prone to relapse. There is a genuine concern that 'those who fail to respond to treatment are likely to face tougher sentences' (Buchanan, 2004: 291). Given that in general female offenders 'appear to struggle with the requirements of court-mandated orders' (Malloch 2004: 229) there is every possibility that more women will be criminalised for offences other than those related to their sex work. Additionally, if the condition of receiving services is that street sex workers seek treatment for drug use, there is a very real possibility that they will stop engaging with support services and much of the good work that is currently being undertaken will be undermined.

The strategy also reminds us that 'drug services are now expected to meet all the drug treatment needs of individuals, whether they are a heroin or crack user, or a poly-drug user, as effective treatment focuses on the client's needs and not just the misuse of the drug' (Home Office, 2006: 44). The strategy recommends that outreach services should be used to encourage women 'to access treatment services and so remove a key motivation for prostitution' (Home Office, 2006: 44) and reminds us that 'the Drug Interventions Programme (DIP) has been developed to use contact between individuals and the criminal justice system as an opportunity to engage with them in a constructive way by assessing their needs, agreeing a care plan and case managing them through appropriate treatment and support' (Home Office, 2006: 44).

Again, providing appropriate services for drug-using sex workers who want to stop using drugs and/or exit sex work is very much to be welcomed. But, as I have noted above, the assumption is that *all* of those involved in street sex work are involved as a result of drug dependence, which is certainly not the case. The measures proposed in the strategy therefore offer very little to street sex workers who are not involved as a result of drug dependence.

By prioritising street sex workers' drug use and drug treatment needs over all other needs the Home Office has ignored the advice and recommendations of its own public consultation exercise. While respondents to the public consultation exercise did acknowledge the importance of providing treatment for those sex workers who are experiencing drug problems and suggested that protocols should be developed for fast-tracking women into immediate assessment and treatment, they did not recommend that women should be coerced into drug treatment through the threat of penal sanctions. A further concern in relation to compelling drug-using sex workers into treatment through the criminal justice system (where extra resources to expand service provision in already overstretched treatment agencies are not available) is that these referrals may displace voluntary clients from drug treatment agencies (Bradley, 1998: 21, cited in Barton, 1999: 475).

The strategy document also asserts that 'dedicated support must be made available wherever there are women trapped in prostitution' (Home Office, 2006: 42). This might be a welcome measure if it were not for the word 'trapped', for once again this implies that when women are involved in sex work they are not acting of their own volition. While this may be true for *some* women it is not universally true, and many women remain engaged in sex work because they do not have realistic alternatives for income generation and, in these circumstances, sex work presents itself as the most viable option.

Where women are 'trapped' in sex work the development of services offering dedicated support is of course most welcome, but once again there is no mention in the prostitution strategy of extra or dedicated resources that would facilitate this development. The strategy recognises that 'it may take some time, and a great deal of support from a dedicated support project, before an individual has the confidence and self-esteem to contemplate treatment and ultimately a route out of street prostitution' (Home Office, 2006: 44). What it does not seem to recognise is that dedicated support projects are mainly provided by NGOs working with very small budgets. This is why, in the consultation exercise, a recommendation was made to provide 'sustained and adequate funding for the provision of long-term, flexible and holistic support' for those involved. While accepting that there is a need for support, the Home Office appears to have ignored the idea that such support needs adequate and sustainable funding. If funding to secure the work of these projects is not to be made available it is difficult to imagine how they might be able to provide the long-term support the Home Office appears to envisage.

The public consultation exercise, while suggesting a need for improved drug treatment services for drug-using sex workers, importantly, did not advocate for these services in isolation from other support. The consultation exercise also acknowledged that many street sex workers are homeless and that housing is a critical issue because 'there are significant difficulties in relation to both capacity and accessibility of suitable housing for this group, particularly for women with mental health and drug addiction problems who continue to sell sex' (Home Office, 2006: 46).

The Home Office itself acknowledges that 'as well as drawing women into street sex work, homelessness can be a critical barrier to exiting' (Home Office, 2006: 46), but appears to have ignored advice that 'a range of accommodation is required to meet the needs at each stage of the exiting process' (Home Office, 2006: 47). Despite recognising that many women involved in street sex work are homeless and/or living in 'drug dens', and that there is a need to ensure 'adequate provision of settled accommodation' if the women concerned are to succeed in finding ways out, there is no mention in the strategy document of money or resources to provide emergency accommodation, safe houses or even more settled accommodation. This suggests that drug-using sex workers are being asked to 'stabilise' their lives by stopping their drug use while they remain in destabilised situations in relation to their housing and economic needs.

Rather than providing extra money or resources for housing, the Home Office looks to the provisions of the 2002 Homelessness Act, under which a person is considered to be in 'priority need' if they are a member of a 'vulnerable' group and they have become homeless through no fault of their own. Involvement in sex work does not automatically render a woman part of a vulnerable group, although she may be deemed to be so if she is fleeing violence, has a mental illness or has been in custody (Home Office, 2006: 47). In these situations accommodation is often provided in hostels. Most of these operate 'zero tolerance' policies in relation to drug use, and if a drug-using sex worker were evicted from a hostel as a result of drug use she would probably be deemed to have made herself homeless voluntarily.

Conclusion

This chapter has argued that one of the major shortcomings of New Labour's 'new' prostitution strategy as it relates to drug-using sex workers is that it mobilises common myths and fictions of addiction. Having mobilised these, it is then able to construct involvement in sex work as an irrational activity driven by chemical compulsion rather than as a rational response to a given set of material and ontological conditions. The strategy reduces involvement in sex work to a problem of drug addiction, then isolates the difficulties experienced by those involved in street sex work and/or problematic drug use from the wider problems of poverty and social exclusion. Rather than treating sex work and/or problematic drug use as inappropriate solutions to the problems of poverty and social exclusion, the strategy treats these phenomena as the problem in itself (see Buchanan, 2004).

The focus on drug addiction as an individual problem 'serves to shift the focus away from socio-structural factors, resulting in a focus on psychological problems as opposed to social circumstances' (Malloch, 2004: 302; Buchanan, 2004). Thus the strategy fails to confront the underlying (structural) conditions that may give rise to involvement in sex work and/or problematic drug use. By insisting that street sex workers enter mandatory drug treatment programmes, the strategy fails to acknowledge the difficulties of changing one's self-identity (for example, as a drug-using sex worker) without changes to the structural and environmental conditions in which the self is subjectively experienced.

A further problem with this new strategy is that sex workers who use drugs tend to be treated as a homogeneous group of 'others' against whom the weight of the criminal justice system can be brought to bear in order to force them to accept the 'help' of drug treatment services. This fails to take account of the many complex (social, health, mental health, educational and economic) problems experienced by these women and fails to understand their drug use and their income-generating activity within the context of specific socio-economic, historical and cultural conditions.

A further limitation of the strategy is that it pays lip service to the welfare needs of drug-using sex workers, because its overarching ambition is to deliver safer communities by removing sex workers from the streets. In this the strategy fails to attend properly to the welfare needs of some of the most vulnerable women and young people in our communities. The strategy document seems to suggest that if delivering community safety involves criminalising vulnerable women and young people who fail to complete court–ordered drug treatment programmes (as many of them surely will) then, 'so be it'.

SIX

Male sex work in the UK: forms, practice and policy implications

Mary Whowell and Justin Gaffney

Introduction

Recent years have witnessed increasing discussion and debate over the changing nature of sex work. Research into street-based sex work has flourished (McKeganey and Barnard, 1996; Hubbard, 2004a: 2004b; Sanders, 2004), while work on the practices, sexualities and spatialities of indoor sex work is becoming more diverse and voluminous (see, *inter alia*, Abbot, 2000 on pornography; Rich and Guidroz, 2000 on telephone sex; Smith, 2002 on stripping; Sanders, 2005 on massage parlours). Despite featuring in the literature on sex work, attention to men who sell sexual services has been notably less than that given to female sex workers. Where present, research on the practices of male sex work has focused on three key themes: sexual health, life histories and methods of entry into the sex industry and, more recently, sex work as a form of erotic labour (Aggleton, 1999; Dorais, 2003; Morrison and Whitehead, 2007).[1] Further, most of this research (both in the UK and internationally) is based on studies of street working. Although these are important topics in their own right, this narrow focus overlooks other important aspects of male sex working, for example, that men work in multiple spaces; that sex work constitutes varied types of body work, performance and companionship as well as penetrative services; and crucially, that men are generally absent from sex work policies, which often purport to be gender neutral. As well as this, much of this research focuses on sex work as being harmful to both worker and client, with little consideration of the benefits or indeed the 'pleasure' afforded in multiple forms that it can bring to some or even all parties. As one male sex worker, Julian, suggests, sex work is not always intrinsically harmful:

> I enjoy my work, I love sex. Okay, I do meet some 'odd' people, but you do in every profession, most of my clients are just normal blokes, looking for some consensual sexual pleasure. For me, like many of them, it's a voyage of discovery.

This chapter highlights some of the progress that has been made in research on male sex work, and will explore the diversity of the male scene. In addition to this, the current policy context in England and Wales will be considered in relation to what is known about patterns, places and forms of male sex work. Supporting evidence will be provided by research and data emanating from the UK, but will also draw on international work.[2] In addition, the authors refer to testimonies from interviews they have undertaken with both men who sell sex and men who buy sex, as part of previous research projects conducted during 2006 and 2007. Further, they cite experiences from front-line agencies (who are members of the UK Network of Sex Work Projects[3]) that have for many years provided outreach, health and social support services to men selling sex.

To develop this, the next section of the chapter will outline the current policy context, paying particular attention to *A Coordinated Prostitution Strategy* (Home Office, 2006). Following this, the chapter then contextualises the male sex industry in terms of its broad demographics and details a new model for thinking about research on male sex work. The next two sections explore different forms and practices of male sex work in public and indoor locations. In the penultimate section of the chapter we return to the policy context. Finally, conclusions will be drawn regarding the current regulation of the male sex industry, and recommendations will be made as to where legislative attention should be focused.

A Coordinated Prostitution Strategy and response to *Paying the Price* – but what about the men?

The Home Office strategy document, *A Coordinated Prostitution Strategy and a summary of responses to 'Paying the Price'* (Home Office, 2006), does focus on the role of men in prostitution, but mainly as abusers of women and children involved in the sex industry, and does so in a way that vilifies men as the perpetrators who drive the sex market. In regards to men selling sex, however, the only substantive mention comes in a narrative at the beginning, when the original consultation document, *Paying the Price: A consultation paper on prostitution* (Home Office, 2004) is

discussed and criticised by respondents for providing 'scant information on male prostitution' (Home Office, 2006: 9). Further, the strategy states that 'the UK Network of Sex Work Projects reports that the majority of men selling sex in the UK are not coerced or trafficked and do not have inappropriate relationships with other individuals who control their movements' (Home Office, 2006: 9). The document goes on to justify why the strategy focuses mainly on the needs of women in prostitution, acknowledging only that it will ensure 'commissioning guidance, and the provision of dedicated support services, addresses the specific needs of these particular groups [men and transgender/transsexual sex workers]'. (Home Office, 2006: 9). Although the strategy claims gender neutrality, there is no substantive analysis of the issues male sex workers may face, or how these issues may be different from (or similar to) those of female sex workers; they are in essence rendered invisible. How, therefore, commissioning guidelines will be developed to address these needs remains a mystery that the strategy document fails to solve. The strategy document outlines five key areas that must be addressed if the issue of prostitution in England and Wales is to be tackled: prevention, tackling demand, developing routes out, ensuring justice and tackling-off street prostitution. In order to address these in terms of male sex working, we must first explore the UK scene and the context of the male sex industry. This will enable us to assess whether the current policy recommendations are applicable, or indeed appropriate, for male sex workers, an issue we address specifically in the final two sections.

Forms and practices of male sex work

In order to conceptualise the workings of the male sex industry, it is important to consider male sex work as existing on a continuum. There are, without doubt, men who have been coerced into and 'damaged' by their involvement in selling sex, often entering street prostitution at an early age. Such experiences are well documented in the literature, and poignant case studies are cited in West and de Villiers (1992). Equally, there are a small number of men who have acquired fame (and fortune) from their public declaration of involvement in the selling of sex (for example, Aiden Shaw[4]). However, as with any distribution within a population, the majority sit somewhere in the middle, just 'normal' men who make a choice to sell sex. Most do it for a short period, most work off street and most would not consider themselves as victims or as having been abused (Ziersch et al, 2000). Brian explains:

There was also a period at secondary school where, because I came from North Yorkshire and went to school in Southampton, I was taken out by various parents of boys, on weekends and things like that and one of the fathers there was actually running a prostitution ring as well. He went to prison for that.

When asked if he felt he had been coerced to provide sexual services to his school friends' fathers, he replies:

I really hadn't been coerced into it, in fact I had asked if I could join in – there's never been coercion for me … basically when you are away from home from age six and a half – I went to boarding school all the way through – you become your own person very rapidly, you learn what makes the world tick, you learn how things go, and as far as I was concerned, sex was an easy way of collecting money, thank you! I enjoyed it so why not? I recognised that I needed sex, why not get paid for having something you enjoy? And this sort of thing of 'everybody's in prostitution because they have a problem', I don't think so. It certainly wasn't with me.

However, some projects report that one of the reasons men become involved in selling sex is rejection from their family or society because of their sexual identity. For example, a Brighton-based study of LGBT (Lesbian, Gay, Bisexual and Transgendered) homeless youth found that up to 20% of the participants (N =44) had sold or exchanged sex for survival purposes (Cull et al, 2006; see also Whowell, 2006). It is important to recognise the complexity of issues and relationships that shape the experiences of men who sell sex, as one Merseyside project manager reports:

Many of the men we work with in Merseyside are very much in control of their own activities yet there are a number of men, who as far as we know are the minority, who are controlled by others, usually using emotional manipulation. There are bigger issues also, homophobia and rejection from sections of the straight community. Also the gay community itself can react negatively and aggressively to men who sell sex. I think this needs to be looked at more.

Most of the published research relating to male sex work demonstrates that many men first start to sell sex before the age of 18 (Connell and Hart, 2003). Yet many also admit to engaging in consensual, non-paid sex before the age of 16 years. It is important to acknowledge that men sell sex for different reasons, at different times of their lives and in very different contexts and spaces.

Although the activity of selling sex for money is a highly individual one, contextualised as it is by individuals' biographies, trajectories, backgrounds and so on, how we understand sex work, that is, the discourse of sex work, has a social specificity that a focus on individual biographies can forget. In this way, the discourse of male sex work, like that of female sex work or prostitution, is historically, politically, legally specific and shaped by other social contexts such as knowledge producing systems – including academic research – and so on. The next section of this chapter provides a model, or overview, of the main themes to have emerged from academic literature since the middle of the 20th century. Through describing the literature in this way, it is possible to trace the ways in which discourses relating to commercial sex shape specific types of policies, interventions and ways of regulating those working in the sex industry.

Researching male sex work

Central to research on male sex workers, like that concerned with female sex workers, has been the construction of an 'identity'. In short, much research on men in the sex industry has been underpinned by the often unstated question: 'What type of man or boy gets involved in sex work?' Perhaps the most commonly cited male sex-working identity within the academic literature is the street hustler (USA) or rent boy (UK). This figure has been a mainstay over the decades but, alongside this, other figures or identities have emerged through progressive academic research, the greater audibility of male sex workers' voices through a variety of media and the greater availability of support services of varying kinds – from support around sexual and mental health to empowerment through union membership. By carefully reviewing the literature on male sex work – especially that emerging from the UK context – it is possible to model or provide an overview of the way in which research on male sex work has developed.[5] The one proposed here focuses on six key themes in the literature.

1. Revolution and revolt

This theme concerns research conducted mainly post–Second World War, until the late 1970s and covering the period when homosexual activity was still illegal (or partially illegal) in the UK. Within this research, young men selling sex were considered to have a psychiatric problem or to be rebellious in their behaviour; their sex work was constituted as being a teenage revolt against society (Deisher et al, 1969; Harris, 1973).

2. Retribution and revenge

This theme concerns research which describes male sex workers as victims, as exemplified in Allen (1980) and Robinson (1989). It dominated research in the 1980s, when much attention was given to young men selling sex from the streets. Within this strand of research, it is suggested that young men selling sex had mostly had troubled backgrounds (for example, they were in care, or subject to family dysfunction, or struggled with drug misuse) and had used sex work as a means to gain control of their sexuality and claim 'revenge' against men for previous abuse.

3. Repressed and revived

This theme describes research that focused almost exclusively on male sex workers as 'the infected' (see, for example, Bloor et al, 1990; Davis and Feldman, 1991) and was conducted from the late 1980s to the early 1990s, when prostitution per se was thought to be a route of HIV transmission into the wider community.

4. Reformed and rebranded

This theme describes research conducted from the mid 1990s to the early 2000s, when there is a notable recognition in research of the wider diversity of men selling sex than was previously imagined. In particular, the focus of research begins to shift away from the types of identities outlined above and from street-based 'rent boys' and starts to focus on off-street work (Hickson et al, 1994; Davis and Feldman, 1997; Thomas, 2000).

5. Rehabilitated and rescued

A new theme in research developed immediately prior to the Home Office consultation document *Paying the Price* (Home Office, 2004). The focus of this new theme is, once again, young men's involvement in sex work, but with this being seen first and foremost as exploitative. Research here implicitly (and at times explicitly) suggests the need to 'rescue' and divert young men away from sex work to other more 'acceptable' activities (see Hudson and Rivers, 2002; Cusick et al, 2003).

6. Recognised and rejuvenated

This theme describes a strand of contemporary discourse of sex work which is underpinned by the recognition of sex work as legitimate labour and that has emerged, arguably, in the context of organised non-sex-work movements affirming or campaigning for the rights and working conditions of sex workers generally (see, for instance, the affiliation by the International Union of Sex Workers (IUSW) to the GMB union) (see Wilcox and Christmann, 2006; Parsons et al, 2007).

These interlinked and overlapping research themes provide a mapping of the ways in which understandings of male sex work and male sex workers have changed over time. However, these themes are by no means monolithic or static, and past research paradigms still infuse current debates in research and policy. For example, *Paying the Price* (Home Office, 2004), the consultation document used to inform *A Coordinated Prostitution Strategy* (Home Office, 2006), was infused with the repressed and revived discourse of the 1990s, which focuses on ideas of sexual health and HIV. The document stated frankly that going to 'prostitutes contributes to the spread of HIV/AIDS and STIs' (Home Office, 2004: 67), an assumption that only serves to perpetuate the notion of 'harm' so often associated with the sex industry.

The following sections explore some of the places and ways in which men sell sex to other men, and the above themes and their applicability to research and policy will be made apparent. The first place to be considered is the street and associated public sex environments (PSEs). Long thought of as being the most traditional place for sex work, this red-light landscape has received much scholarly attention (Harris, 1973; Davis and Feldman, 1991; Barnard, 1993; Connell and Hart, 2003; Hubbard and Whowell, 2008), but here we draw on current examples from our own research on the UK scene (see also Gaffney and Beverly, 2001). Thereafter we turn to 'off street' environments, as the majority of men involved in selling sex in the UK do so from private flats and apartments, or through the use of new technologies, such as the internet and web-cams.

Working the 'meat rack' – the street and public sex

Many of the UK services that work with the small number of young men selling sex on the street would recognise the retribution and revenge theme in research, as this does reflect the personal situation of many young men who work the street beats[6] in the UK. Some street-working men (like street-working women) use drugs, solvents and alcohol, and are involved in the street-related criminality that has links to drug culture (Connell and Hart, 2003). The Armistead Project in Merseyside reports that this pattern of problematic drug use, and the need to sell or exchange sex for drugs, is an issue among some young gay and bisexual men selling sex. The Merseyside project also reports having worked with heterosexually identified men who sell sex to support their heroin use. Other projects outside Merseyside also recount similar issues, such as the Male Sex Worker Outreach Project (MSWOP) in Manchester. In central London, on the other hand, a slightly different issue is noted. Central London Action on Street Health (CLASH) and the Working Men Project (WMP) have commented that many of their clients and other street-based male sex workers are addicted to crack-cocaine, and that selling sex is part of their wider criminal portfolio, which includes mugging, clipping, pimping (their female partners), shop- lifting and car theft. In contrast again, in Southampton young men who would traditionally be considered as part of the street sex-work scene have also been found to be working in semi-public spaces. Barnardo's (a children's charity) works with young men involved in diverse sectors of the industry, including those who have become entangled in pornography, organised sex parties (whereby guests will pay a fee and then the sex will be 'free of charge' on the premises), those exchanging sex in PSEs and also those who seek clients via the internet. Here, new technologies have had a major impact on the forms and practices of male sex work, with mobile phones and the web being identified as the key methods used by boys to meet up with clients. The importance of this is that both these forms of technology serve to disguise the networks and places in which young boys are involved in selling sex, and thus increase the requirement for innovative and effective service provision (J. Wright, Barnardo's Southampton, personal communication, 2008). This work specifically with young people who are in danger of exploitation through the sex industry reflects the wider proliferation of work into services for young people (boys and girls) at risk of sexual exploitation (Hudson and Rivers, 2002) and is underpinned by the construction of a young male sex worker as in need of rehabilitation and rescue. That said, we are not suggesting that the interventions based on such notions are not life changing and/or they do not have a positive effect on the lives of young people exploited through prostitution.

Despite evidence from services and academic research, it is not the case that most adult men and young men working from the streets suffer from problematic drug use, are criminal and have multiple and complex needs. Reports from one northern city suggest that some young men working the beat feel victimised – not by exploiters, but by the police. Simply stated, many young men working from the streets are often suspected of being involved in street crime when in fact they are not – when they are merely selling sex. As Carl suggests:

> They [the police] should ... help us instead of being against us because that's how I feel that they are doing, that they are against us at the moment because they think, 'they're all scum, they're on drugs or they're doing this, they're doing that' but not all of us are doing robberies or things like that. We've been through a harsh time so I think we've got to make money some other way.

In other words, the street scene may well be much more diverse than previous research suggests, and certainly more diverse than is implied by the stereotype of the 'rougher and tougher' street sex worker. It would seem that male sex workers perform their work in an ever-expanding multiplicity of ways. The (as yet unrecognised) diversity of the street scene has implications in terms of the way in which it is regulated at present. *A Coordinated Prostitution Strategy* (Home Office, 2006) takes an enforcement approach in which one of the central loci of intervention is through criminal justice responses to prostitution-related offences, especially soliciting, loitering and kerb crawling. Hence, tackling kerb crawling is a central component of the strategy on tackling demand, yet using this method of enforcement against male street sex workers is complex and problematic and these complexities are not considered in the strategy. Nearly all street-based male sex working occurs in well-known areas (streets or PSEs as described above). Here men are often approached on foot by men seeking to purchase their services. However, what the above suggests – which is reflected in a dated ethnographic description of the male sex-worker street scene (see Harris, 1973) – is that the rich tapestry of the urban cityscape can *conceal* much male sex work. Yet, only one section of *A Coordinated Prostitution Strategy* refers to 'punters on foot', who, it is suggested, 'must be prosecuted rigorously to protect local communities from the nuisance that their behaviour causes to reduce the demand for a street sex market' (Home Office, 2006: 35). Such a premise is seriously flawed in regard to the male sex-work scene. It is not unusual for men to congregate together, and often the male sex-working scene can be found either in busy pedestrianised city centres, with bars, shops and cafes that provide cover for the activities that occur, or in known cruising areas and public sex environments, where commercial sexual activities mingle unnoticed with other routine social interaction. It is rare that such communities will even be aware of the sex-working scene, or any nuisance related to PSE activities, as opposed to the selling of sex per se.

As well as this, those men who, in order to fund drug or alcohol addiction/abuse, for instance, are involved in more traditional criminal activities alongside street-based sex work often find that they are more likely to be arrested for those criminal activities rather than for soliciting or loitering. Intervention at this point in relation to their sex work is seldom offered, and many men may feel uncomfortable disclosing their sex work activity. This may especially be the case if the sex worker identifies as heterosexual, as there may also be issues around sexuality to be considered.

Evidence from sex-work projects across the UK suggests that the majority of men who sell sex are likely to be those who sell sex *occasionally* to meet specific economic needs. Indeed, Billy, who works primarily in public places, has 'exited' sex work a number of times, yet he will often return to the beat to make some fast cash when he feels like it. 'It's easy money, it's like I say, you can end up with more money than you would do from benefits, from even a job.'

For some, exchanging sex for money may be only an occasional or opportunistic event. Public sex environments provide a transient and somewhat ambiguous venue for young men to experiment with their sexualities. A PSE can be described as any public space in which men engage in sexual acts anonymously with other men in public (yet usually discreet) spaces (Correlation Network, 2008). Such spaces can include country roads, shops, toilets, canal paths, swimming pools, parks, cinemas, roads, clubs, bars, beaches and car parks (Gaffney, 2002; see also Bell, 2001; Atkins, 2007). The accessibility of the PSE – especially given that information on where they are and even details on who will be there is available on the internet – can provide a relatively comfortable and, at times, unexpected introduction to sex work for some young men:

> PSE's [sic] and the street are often used by younger gay men, and gay/bisexual men who are coming to terms with their sexuality and using such environments as places of experimentation. In doing so, such young men may be approached by older gay men who are seeking to buy sex, who may offer this younger man money or favours in exchange for sex. The young men [sic] may capitalise on this opportunity, and realise that he has the ability to sell sex and begin to develop sex selling skills. Street scenes may have a local reputation for being places where sex is sold, which may be the initial draw of the young men. (Gaffney, 2002: 18)

The PSE therefore poses a major challenge to service providers, outreach workers and early intervention teams when it comes to negotiating the places and spaces through which men sell sex, and also accessing young men who may not associate their actions with those of someone who sells or exchanges sex. This is especially poignant for those men who use the PSE to exchange sex and also have little or no contact with wider social networks or the commercial gay scene, as the outreach service may be their only access point for help or information on safer sexual exchange (WMP, 2003).

Despite the continued use of PSEs and also more traditional street beats, there is no doubt that much male sex work is moving off-street and being replaced by a series of indoor spaces and transient networks facilitated by technological advances. The Working Men Project (2006) in London has suggested that it was primarily the deregulation of the telecommunications industry in the 1990s and the advent of the 'pay as you go' mobile that helped this shift. In addition, the increased availability of public internet access in cafes and libraries allows men to cruise for paying partners on the web and get in touch via email or telephone to organise encounters off-street. The sheer diversity of male sex work provided through these technological changes sits at odds with the rather simplistic understanding of public sex work as evidenced in *A Coordinated Prostitution Strategy*.

'Indoor' modes of sex working

This section discusses forms and practices of sex work that occur off-street and beyond the public sphere. It is worth noting at this stage that many men, especially those who work in the industry for a prolonged period of time, will move between sectors and also operate in semi-public places of encounter such as baths, saunas, clubs and bars, and that this fluidity of movement is something that has become increasingly evident since the 1990s – largely as a result of the development of research and activist networks (see also Morrison and Whitehead, 2007). Evidence from London suggests that some independent escorts working from their own or rented flats may have previously worked on the street, in massage parlours or brothels, and will sometimes move around the industry (Gaffney, 2002). Discussion in this section draws on research underpinned by a notion of the male sex worker as reformed and rebranded, and as recognised and rejuvenated (as discussed earlier).

Mostly, men sell sex to other men off-street and behind closed doors. The most 'visible' element of this commercial male scene is the advertisements for escorts in the gay media, but even these are contained in publications advertising themselves as having 'adult sexual content', and so are not usually accessed widely by 'mainstream' society. Brothels tend to be managed, discreet and orderly, and located in neighbourhoods where they 'blend in' to a busy street scene, so a stream of workers or clients entering and leaving the premises throughout the day will pass largely unnoticed. Often escorts will simply provide company for their clients, they may provide partial or full sexual services, or specialise in role-play or fetish sex play. Others will cater for particular sexual tastes or fantasies, or provide erotic massage. Indeed there is now more than ever an increasing number of men and women who work with disabled clients.[7]

The organised commercial scene is self-regulating around the protection of young people. Brothels often seek clarification in the form of documentation (birth certificates, passports) to confirm the age of new men wanting to work at the premises. Magazines and internet sites that host photographs and advertisements or listings also have similar checks and will want to confirm that the pictures of the person placing the advert or listing are genuine. Indeed, it has been the experience of projects in the UK Network of Sex Work Projects (UKNSWP) that men selling sex independently are often known to social services on the basis of reporting potential child abuse concerns. This is an important point not considered in *A Coordinated Prostitution Strategy* – that male (and female) sex workers and those who work with them (including managers, maids and drivers) are regulators of the sex industry, and are possibly in the best position to report those who are at risk of abuse. As well as this, older sex workers are often the best advocates for dissuading young people from choosing sex work as an option or, where they do, ensuring that they develop survival and work skills to conduct business safely and maintain appropriate boundaries, notably emotional boundaries, with paying partners (McKinney and Gaffney, 2000; Ziersch et al, 2000).

The desire to develop good work skills and to learn how to improve business standards in order to attract more customers may be due to increased competition in UK (but especially London-based) markets (Gaffney, 2002). Such negotiation around working practices reflects the shifts noted in the literature, and in particular the shift towards the recognition and rejuvenation of male sex workers as legitimate workers (Parsons et al, 2007). As one escort explains, 'you have to basically market yourself, find a way to market yourself, and deliver what you say you'll deliver. I send thank-you notes to my clients. I'm literally a customer service business' (quoted in Parsons et al, 2007: 226). Creating and maintaining a professional business approach towards work as a way to fight off competition also raises issues around time management. The saturated London market has meant that many workers cannot afford to miss a client if their services are requested. Men are often on call 24 hours a day as a result, and have to plan personal life around being close to their space of work (usually also their home) in case a call comes in from a client (Gaffney, 2002). This lifestyle can be extremely stressful and has the potential to provoke frustration, job dissatisfaction and even mental health issues (see Gaffney, 2002). As exampled by Marco:

> Computer on 24 hours, I have my commercial Gaydar[8] profile and if I don't have a message, I go in the escort/ client room which is the only way to send messages to the client. I send messages to those in London looking for boys and when I'm lucky I get a client a day, sometimes two, sometimes none ... This is my life, television, eat, listen to music, stand in front of the computer. All day. It's not very nice.

Revisiting the policy context

The above sections give a general overview of the context and social organisation of male sex work in England and Wales. This final section draws together some of the key issues vis-à-vis regulation for men working in the sex industry and also the implications for their clients. As an organising principle, this section takes each strand of *A Coordinated Prostitution Strategy* (Home Office, 2006) and explores specific consequences of its implementation for men in the sex industry.

Prevention

In *A Coordinated Prostitution Strategy*, prevention is focused on raising awareness of violence, vulnerability and exploitation in prostitution and advocating early intervention to prevent individuals, particularly young men and women, from entering prostitution. The strategy does not distinguish between the sexes, yet there are clear distinctions between the experiences of young men and young women involved in prostitution, as the above bears witness. Young men selling sex are often seen as 'delinquent' rather than vulnerable, so the needs and potential exploitation of younger men tend to be unseen by researchers, policy makers and official agencies. There is undoubtedly an underground crime scene in relation to children and younger men which may include trafficked boys; this is not something condoned by the well-regulated adult commercial male scene and occurs separately from it. Violence is less prevalent in the male scene, but in regard to the violence that does occur, some men may be reluctant to report assault, as they would also have to disclose their sex working and hence be vulnerable to stigma associated with male sexual crime. However, violence for street-working men is a reality, although this is often related to their problematic drug or alcohol use or homelessness, rather than to involvement in the selling of sex (Connell and Hart, 2003). The potential for men to experience violence in the sex industry is not recognised in the strategy, although it is well reported by the UKNSWP that sex-work projects do work with men on issues around staying safe (see UKNSWP, 2008).

Tackling demand

This area of the strategy focuses on street prostitution, and in particular on shifting the emphasis of legislation away from criminalising the sex worker for soliciting and loitering and towards criminalising the sex purchaser. While there have been regular calls to criminalise the purchasing of sex per se, *A Coordinated Prostitution Strategy* has shaped a renewed focus on the enforcement of the law on kerb crawling, and a staged approach to enforcement against loitering or soliciting. Central to this objective was an anti-kerb-crawling campaign launched by the Home Office in May 2007 in seven cities in England – with the tag line 'kerb-crawling costs more than you think'. Media used to implement the campaign and advertise the tag line included beer mats and posters, and radio 'warnings'. This campaign, focused as it was on demonising, ruining, shaming and disgracing clients, worked through playing on notions of what is deemed to be appropriate sexual behaviour and what is seen to be inappropriate, 'deviant' or 'immoral' sexual behaviour, that is, purchasing sex (Sanders, 2008a). Research shows, however, that men who purchase sex from either men or women are, in the main, respectful of sex workers, non-violent, and practise safe sex; and in some cases intimate relationships between clients and workers can develop (Sanders, 2008a). *A Coordinated Prostitution Strategy* is also unclear on defining what is understood by 'purchasing sex' and the intent that is associated with this consensual exchange. In other words, there is the implication underpinning the UK's present direction of regulation that 'purchasing sex' somehow calls into question the issue of consent to the sexual activities that take place. While this may generate a set of debates for women, the issues for men are perhaps a little less complex. Not only is the selling and purchasing of sex integrally interconnected with contemporary gay cultures and communities, sex work for many adult men is also bound up with their sexuality, with leisure and pleasure, as well as with economic exchanges. As Richard, a man who buys sex (from men, but identifies as heterosexual), explained:

> Um, there is no real difference between [paying another man for sex, and] me taking my – when it was girlfriend – taking her out, me picking her up in a fancy car, bunch of flowers, taking her out to the theatre, having a snog in the back then going out for dinner somewhere, champagne, get a bit pissed, have another brandy here, and go home, and then have sex – costs an arm and leg but you see I am purchasing that, the evening was planned, with the intent for sex!

The proposition to criminalise the purchasing of sex in the context of the male sex industry puts in place a regulatory system that is not dissimilar to that which existed prior to the legalisation of homosexuality and when consensual adult sexual relations were seen to require intervention from the state in order to remain within the realms of 'morality'. This had devastating effects on individuals and on the gay community. So, for instance, the playwright Oscar Wilde was famously punished by such laws on account of his intimate relationship with Alfred 'Bosie' Douglas and their rumoured flirtations with rent boys at the time. Imprisoned and forced to do two years' 'hard labour', Wilde suffered illness from living in squalid conditions. Following his release, Wilde spent the last three years of his life with friends and living in cheap hotels in Europe, and died in November 1900 of meningitis.[9] Modern-day comparisons (with less severe consequences) can be made. The scandal involving Mark Oaten, Liberal Democrat Home Affairs spokesman and his six-month affair with a 'rent boy' in 2006 caused him to stand down from the party's leadership contest (BBC, 2006). The media reported that he was someone 'who has been elected on a platform of being a family man'. His association as a client stripped him of this reputation (BBC, 2006; see also Kulick, in press, on the Ronaldo scandal, involving three *travesti*[10] sex workers in April 2008).

What is at stake here is not that criminalisation of privately enacted sexual transactions between consenting adults would add criminal prosecution to the humiliation and disgrace that often accompanies being 'found out' as a male client of a male sex worker. Rather, the very precepts of the Wolfenden Report and the liberalisation of the laws regarding homosexuality and prostitution, that is, that the law had no place in regulating questions of sexual morality for consenting adults, would be seriously undermined. Again, Richard comments:

> It sounds ludicrous to me, unworkable, ultimately unworkable, and the worst thing possible is to push it underground, perhaps because it will lead to the more furtive past – what a bad time ... And I can't think that it does any harm other than resentment that some old guys are still getting sex when most of society might feel they should stop such things!

In short, the drive to tackle demand through criminal justice responses against either male sex workers or their clients is something that is likely to impact severely and negatively not just on many gay individuals, but on the gay community itself.

Developing routes out

Implementing exiting schemes for male sex workers is an extremely complex task, and analysis of some of these issues shows up another conceptual and strategic difficulty with *A Coordinated Prostitution Strategy*. The assumption within the strategy is that 'exiting' prostitution is a linear and, more importantly, easily identified process, and that individual sex workers actually want to 'exit' from a profession that is currently legal. Indeed, these assumptions are themselves informed by the construction of sex workers as in need of rehabilitation and rescue. Much of the work around exiting, or indeed developing routes out of, prostitution focuses on moving *women* away from prostitution, through education and training, to other forms of employment deemed to be more appropriate. While the notion of 'exiting' may in principle have beneficial effects for men who sell sex, starting from the premise that the activity they are engaged in is 'wrong' and that they need directing along a more acceptable pathway may only ensure their disengagement. For the sex worker who may not be breaking any laws through their work practice, the notion of 'needing to exit' is a problematic one, as is the case of the sex worker who wants to exit but who may require appropriate support and intervention for many months and even years after leaving sex work. It is not clear how this will be provided for men across England and Wales, as the commissioning guidelines on advising how to do this are as yet unavailable.

More than anything else, however, the requirement for people involved in the sex industry to follow specific routes out of prostitution is unrealistic. Evidence from SohoBoyz and SW5 (both London-based services for male sex workers) has found that using a more organic approach can often be successful in helping men move away from selling sex. Offering support and providing men with the opportunity to make informed choices about working in the sex industry through non-judgemental and supportive means has the potential to enable men to make positive choices about their involvement in sex work, which can include adopting safer working practices or exit. Through this process, the men engaging with the project are able to reach a position whereby they have greater agency and a heightened ability to make proactive life-style choices. Programmes that develop a greater 'professionalism' in the sex work being undertaken and that seek to develop the entrepreneurial skills of sex-working men ensure engagement, while facilitating the acquisition of new skills (financial management, negotiation, marketing and so on) that are 'transferable' and may provide opportunities beyond the selling of sex.

Ensuring justice

This element of the strategy outlines plans to use current legislation to bring justice to those involved in exploiting individuals through prostitution and those who commit violence and sexual offences against people involved in prostitution. Violence from clients is very rare with off-street male sex workers. Nevertheless, the murder of a male masseur in London in 2004 suggests that they may share some of the vulnerabilities of female sex workers operating alone. As one male sex worker states: 'the major advantage [of] working as an escort at an agency is the safety issue. Many boys[11] feel a sense of security working in a house, whereas boys working privately or working out-calls tend to feel unsafe' (interview, 2006). Boys who work as escorts often use the sex industry as an opportunity to make quick and easy money, but understand that risk comes as part of that work.

Escorts will often seek to learn how to manage the risks they may encounter in the first instance, rather than rely on protection from the law. This highlights issues of protection and justice as complex; the notion of the government seeking to prosecute those who abuse or 'control' sex workers is, in principle, useful. If those who are violent towards sex workers, those who manage sex businesses poorly, or those who are involved in underground economies were removed from the industry, the law would go some way to ensuring the safety of sex workers. However, such laws could (quickly) become dangerous if the meanings of words such as 'control' were not explicitly defined. The implementation of poorly thought-out rulings could result in maids or sex-business managers who work for the best interests of sex workers being prosecuted for 'control', or for details such as setting prices for services or arranging safe, secure transportation between appointments. Although the notion of 'ensuring justice' has value, it must also ensure justice for those working in the sex industry, and must not be used to scapegoat or prosecute sex workers. Better regulation of the industry, and recognition at both policy and legislative levels that sex workers have the right to work safely, and with recourse to police support in cases of threat, attack or fraudulent payments for their services, would ensure a far greater sense of justice.

Tackling off-street prostitution

The organisation of off-street male sex work was discussed earlier. In addition, however, it is worth noting that since 1997 only one London-based male brothel has been closed by the police and its owners successfully prosecuted. Yet even in this case, the charges on which the owners were given custodial sentences pertained to unpaid tax (from the brothel) rather than to running a male brothel. Brothels that front as 'unlicensed massage parlours' are generally well run and the men working in them do so voluntarily. Off-street male sex work does not seem to have the same problems of violence, trafficking and exploitation that are assumed to be prevalent for female sex workers.

Perhaps the greatest problem relating to off-street prostitution for men is isolation and, unlike for their female colleagues, for whom isolation (working alone in flats) can lead to an increased risk of violence and sexual assault, isolation creates a problem of 'barriers' and 'stigma'. Given that the majority of adult males selling sex in the UK identify as gay (and even where they identify as hetero- or bisexual), because most men sell sex to other men, they can face discrimination and homophobia as a result of their involvement in sex work. Such discrimination, real or perceived, can be a barrier to accessing services. Furthermore, project workers have reported that many male sex workers in London are from outside the UK. Often these are men who identify as gay or bisexual, arrive in the UK on a holiday or student visa, and find the relatively tolerant society and established gay scene liberating and become reluctant to leave. This is especially the case for those men who come from small urban or rural communities with traditional Catholic values. This group of men may turn to sex work in order to fund an extended stay. Because English is often not their first language, they can experience problems entering sex work through this route and accessing services or wider gay communities. In addition to being gay and a migrant worker, many male sex workers face additional stigma from being involved in the sex industry. Finally, as discussed earlier, increased competition between sex workers can cause stress; the driving down of prices can force male workers to constantly have to negotiate what they are willing to provide in terms of services in order to secure business, and also increase working hours. In this way, the problems that need tackling in regard to off-street male sex work are quite different from those evidenced in regard to off-street female sex work.

Conclusion

This chapter has sought to highlight some difficulties that the current direction of prostitution policy in England and Wales (Home Office, 2006) has in terms of its applicability to men working in the sex industry. There is little doubt that it fails to address many of the key issues that male sex workers face. What this chapter has demonstrated is that, contrary to assumptions contained within current policy, the off-street male sex markets, which constitute the largest proportion of the male sex industry in the UK, are already effectively self-regulating against exploitation. If there is to be government attention to men working in the sex industry, then perhaps it should focus on raising standards of practice in the adult industries. This could, for example, include codes of safer working practice for pornographic artists, banning bareback sex

(sex without a condom), or the introduction of training programmes for those working in the sex industry so that they know how to remain happy, safe and healthy. In addition, the proposed criminalisation of the purchase of consensual sexual activity has the potential (from a male sex-work perspective) to take gay liberation back 50 years and increase the vulnerability to bribery, corruption and exploitation of both the men who sell sex and those who purchase it; and in essence, it could push the activity underground. The authors posit that the organisation of the off-street commercial male sex industry within England and Wales should be cited as an example of 'best practice' for the decriminalisation of sex work in general, and that lessons could be learned from this sector to improve the working conditions and the health and safety of the female sex industry through organisation of industry stakeholders and application of the self-regulatory principles practised within the male industry.

Notes

[1] Although see also Bimbi (2007).

[2] Much of the data used to inform this chapter emanate from original research completed by the authors. This includes data from Whowell's PhD thesis, and research completed by Gaffney in conjunction with sex-work agencies and networks.

[3] The UK Network of Sex Work Projects (UKNSWP) is a non-profit, voluntary association of agencies and individuals working with sex workers. See www.uknswp.org for more information.

[4] Aiden Shaw is a multi-award-winning British-born pornographic actor who has starred in over 50 adult films. He is also the author of several published works, including semi-autobiographical books and poetry.

[5] See Bimbi (2007) for an alternative mapping.

[6] The 'beat' is another term for a street in which men or women sell sex. Areas exclusive to young men selling sex are also often referred to as the 'meat rack'.

[7] See www.tlc-trust.org.uk

[8] Gaydar is an online networking site for gay and bisexual men and hosts commercial profiles for sex workers.

[9] See www.cmgww.com/historic/wilde/index.php for more information.

[10] *Travesti* in Brazil are males who prefer to engage in female behaviour, in terms of dress, mannerisms and attributes. They are not transgendered in the sense of sex change, as they retain their penis, and often work in the sex industry. Although *travesties* may have all the defining characteristics of women, they never define as women – they define as males. See Kulick (in press) for more on this.

[11] The generic industry term for a male sex worker; it does not refer to an individual under 18 years old.

SEVEN

Beyond child protection: young people, social exclusion and sexual exploitation

Jenny Pearce

Introduction

In this chapter I make two key points about service delivery for sexually exploited children and young people. First, I argue that while there have been some helpful developments in policy and practice that raise the profile of sexually exploited children and young people's needs (HM Government, 2008b; DCSF, 2008), these have mainly been focused on child protection agendas. Other considerations, such as the housing needs of young people, their education and training needs and their health needs have been overlooked. Despite Local Safeguarding Children Boards being multi-agency, the focus has remained on child protection issues, leaving many sexually exploited young people, particularly 16- to 18-year-olds, without access to the full range of service provision to which they are entitled. I therefore argue that there needs to be a shift in the locus of intervention. Second, I argue that, as a consequence of the focus on child protection, sexually exploited children and young people are seen first and foremost as victims of abuse. This dominant definition hides other important aspects of the child's identity. I therefore provide an analysis of sexual exploitation that does not reify the young person's experiences of victimisation, but that locates 'the problem' of sexual exploitation as a social welfare problem.

A background context

In the mid 1970s I attended a memorable feminist conference on rape and domestic violence against women. For me, the most powerful talk was by an established and well-respected practitioner/academic who referred to the fact that she herself had been a victim of rape, noting the trauma and the damage that it had caused. However, her point was that, while she had been a victim of rape, she had fought to prevent herself from becoming a victim for the rest of her life. She compared the impact of the rape on her life with the deep significance that her mother's death had had, and explained that, in her view, each individual reconstructs the impact of a tragedy on their life in ways personal to them. There is no one event, such as rape, domestic violence or, indeed, sexual exploitation, that can ever universally be claimed to be the 'worst' thing that can ever happen to someone. Similarly, there can be no one definition of 'victim' that can encompass the way that different people respond. The core theme emerging from the conference was that women who had experienced violence and abuse could have their own sense of agency undermined if they were grouped together under an all-encompassing 'victim' label. The now very familiar argument was made that women would experience and understand the impact of violence in their lives in different ways and that they could take some control and be 'survivors'. They could use support structures to lead active lives and maintain healthy relationships. There was no denial that there were casualties, but the overriding challenge was to prevent the identity of victim being superimposed over and above other identities.

Similarly, children and young people who have experienced sexual exploitation have a central, important voice in constructing the meaning that the abuse has made in their lives. The challenge to policy makers working to protect children and young people from sexual exploitation is to create a framework within which the child or young person is protected, at the very same time as giving the young person a say in how they want to define themself. This means encouraging the child or young person to have access to supported housing, to health services and to develop their own education and training. So I argue that while *A Coordinated Prostitution Strategy* (and also the Department of Children, Schools and Families' updated version [DCSF, 2008] of the original *Safeguarding Children Involved in Prostitution Guidance* [DH, 2000]) is right to place the sexual exploitation of children and young people under a child protection focus in children's services, there is an unexplored and associated concern that, by default, the young person becomes seen only as a victim of abuse.

Sexual exploitation and sexual abuse

Before I explore this in detail, I want to clarify that I am not suggesting that we return to the days when young people were processed through criminal justice procedures for offences relating to prostitution. What I am proposing is that 'protection' is only one part of the overall picture. While sexually exploited children and young people should remain on the safeguarding agenda, this should not be the only locus of intervention; indeed, for some young people it need not be the main locus of intervention. Sexually exploited young people have peer-group associations, aspirations to achieve in education or work, and a desire to take part in leisure activities just as any others their age. They may also be rebellious, challenging and difficult in the same way as many other young people will be. Many will not conform to a victim label and will challenge acceptance of the need for protection. Research has shown that some sexually exploited young people, particularly those who have been groomed over a long period of time and/or who have serious problems with drug dependency, may be extremely damaged and vulnerable. It has also shown that many try to take control over their lives and make choices in how they develop their future, albeit choices 'constrained' by the limited opportunity available to them (Melrose and Barrett, 2004; Pearce, 2006).

Traditionally, child protection services have been established to protect children and young people from familial sexual abuse. These services are not always equipped to respond to the complex and diverse needs of older sexually exploited young people (Coy, 2006). The reality for many local authority children's services is that they have to provide a reactive service, responding with limited resources to meet extensive demand. The plethora of child abuse inquiries has revealed services struggling to protect the most vulnerable children in the home. The fear of becoming the next authority to hit the press for failing to protect a child encourages a focus on early family interventions and on the movement of young children from abusive family circumstances. This is understandable. However, if children's services are to take responsibility for keeping *all* children safe (HM Government, 2008b), for helping all young people to achieve their full potential (HM Government, 2003) and for safeguarding them from sexual exploitation (DH, 2000; DCSF, 2008), certain developments in delivery to teenagers, to those who will soon be 18, in employment and living independently, need to take place.

Also, as reviews of practice and research have shown, many of these young people do not ask to be protected. They may openly rebel against being seen as victims, may have been groomed by people they call 'friends', may proclaim 'love' for their abuser, may be in a complicated, interdependent violent relationship with an abuser, or may be purposefully swapping or selling sex for accommodation, food, drugs or money. As noted by a recent evaluation of services:

> All these young people present three major challenges to services attempting to intervene in their lives. First, they do not acknowledge their own exploitation. Second, they are extremely 'needy' for attention, 'love' and of belonging somewhere – and are reliant on abusive adults to meet these needs. Third, they have little previous experience of adult support and believe they are better off looking after themselves rather than relying on parents or professionals. (Scott and Skidmore, 2006: 3)

To meet this range of issues in a way that fosters trust and empowers the young person to build positively on the strengths and resilience they have already demonstrated, we need a child protection service that is fully integrated with employment, distance-learning training activities, health and leisure activities, therapeutic outreach services, and police. Indeed, to take this to its logical conclusion, we need youth services to be better integrated with child protection services so that they can access and engage with the young people concerned out on their estates, on their streets and in close proximity to where they are staying/living at the time.

However, there is a long way to go before integrated responses managed through safeguarding children boards and involving youth service providers can meet the complex needs of adolescents; build their confidence in their own agency, their self-determination; and listen to their voices describing the impact that sexual exploitation has had, and will have, on their development. If and when we do listen to the young person, we often hear stories of struggles against social exclusion, poverty, and marginalisation from mainstream services (Scott and Harper, 2006). What this means is that we have to take poverty seriously when developing policy to protect sexually exploited young people. I will discuss this in more detail below, before moving on to suggest how social work child protection services can work with housing, training, employment and domestic violence services to support the young people concerned.

Poverty, social exclusion and youth transition

The spatial entrapment and social exclusion that can be caused by poverty (that is, the lack of opportunity to move easily from one or two local streets, to engage in the commercial world in ways that are portrayed through general advertising, television and film, to access or achieve at school and work) are key features that many young people contend with in their transition to adulthood. Young people can be particularly vulnerable to marginalisation from mainstream services, and to sexual exploitation if this is accompanied by a familial or peer-group engagement with informal economies, with problem drug or alcohol misuse, or with previous experiences of abuse. This is not to suggest that, to be truly damaging, poverty needs to be accompanied by familial or personal pathologies. To suggest this would place the emphasis on individuals and their families rather than on the structural inequalities that they have to contend with.

Many studies of poverty and social exclusion have tended to focus on the individual capabilities of excluded persons rather than to address the changing social and economic conditions that impact upon them. Shildrick and MacDonald (2008: 45) look at the interplay between 'individual agency, local (sub) cultures and the social structural context'. Their work notes that to focus on one of these aspects to the exclusion of others provides only one-third of the story. If we are to fully embrace the reasons why an individual young person is sexually exploited, the social and economic context within which that individual resides must be addressed. Of course, both poverty and social exclusion are complex issues, well established over many generations in debates about the sale of sex and exploitation of children (Crosby and Barrett, 1997; Pitts, 1997; Self, 2003). The fact that poverty, and the social exclusion that accompanies it, are so hard to challenge can mean that it is easier to construct policy around individual redemption rather than to engage with efforts to create larger-scale structural change.

This dilemma is not new. Indeed, in 1885 child prostitution was defined as a 'veritable slave trade', where individual children were

> snared, trapped and outraged either when under the influence of drugs or after a prolonged struggle in a locked room. (Stead, 1885, cited in Gorham, 1978: 353)

Interventions then tended to focus on 'saving' the individual young women from harm rather than on challenging the poverty those individuals experienced. Motivated to rescue young women from prostitution, Stead raised considerable attention to the plight of young women who were moved from their homes, and in some cases taken into Europe to work in brothels. His work did, however, note the impact that poverty had on young women, who could easily fall into a situation of debt bondage, and showed how financial dependency often existed between the young person and a (usually older male) adult. In 1884 Josephine Butler, Bramwell Booth of the Salvation Army and other reformers focused on the relationship between sex, money and social class, noting that it was younger women of working-class origins who were entering prostitution. This relationship was highly gendered, and was then, as it is now, manifest in social practices and the resulting social interventions targeted at young women.

Although sexual exploitation and social exclusion were not the discourses of the time, the work of the reformers and the associated literature explored the way in which sex becomes a currency when few, if any, other currencies are available. However, as argued, despite poverty being noted as a significant contributing factor, much of the response at the time was focused on 'rescuing' the individuals concerned rather than on addressing the poverty that they experienced. Exploring this in more depth, Self (2003) addresses the difficulty facing the reformers of the 1880s. She notes their desire to both protect girls, the object of their concern, and control them. On the one hand there was the aim to rescue and care for the innocent girl, while on the other hand there was the difficulty of managing the young person's behaviour. If her behaviour did not change, or if she did not show herself as deserving of support through her good behaviour, she was penalised for wayward immorality as a sexually active young woman. Indeed, it could be argued that the last two centuries of policy on troubled and troubling children has been constituted by the fundamental contradiction between the desire to care and the demand to control (Phoenix, 2002). Gorham (1978) notes the inherent contradictions in the Victorian era between rescuing the deserving poor from destitution, on the one hand, and penalising the 'promiscuous' undeserving reoffender on the other, showing how the desire to rescue girls, who were, in almost all cases, young working-class children, was influenced by whether or not the girls conformed to sexual stereotypes. In a campaign that aimed to appeal to the 'righteousness of all decent people', she noted:

> In much of the reform rhetoric, the young prostitutes are portrayed as sexually innocent, passive victims of individual evil men. This imagery of individual sin, with its corresponding possibility of individual redemption, may have been comforting to these late-Victorian middle class reformers. (Gorham, 1978: 355)

If we now move on in time, to 2000, we see similar contradictions within the existing government guidance for safeguarding children involved in prostitution (DH, 2000). The Department of Health's (2000) guidance made it clear that a young person should be supported through child protection services, unless they 'persistently and voluntarily' return to prostitution. If they do, they can be penalised through the criminal justice system for offences relating to prostitution. Anecdotal evidence is beginning to suggest that even if the young person is not penalised through the use of offences related to prostitution, they are being dealt with through anti-social behaviour measures. This is despite increasing concern among many social researchers that the focus on young people's anti-social behaviour develops a 'blame' culture, shifting attention onto the individual child's behaviour and away from the social and economic context they find themselves in.

> There has been too much emphasis on anti-social behaviour and too ready willingness to attribute blame either to parents or to young people themselves. (Coleman and Scofield, 2007: xi)

In other words, the child is blame-free when acting as a victim of abuse, but blamed when 'acting out' against it. The child can be supported as a victim, but criminalised when rebelling against the label. This is despite much of the research suggesting that those who are the most challenging and who do persistently return to selling sex are the most disadvantaged, the most damaged and the most in need of welfare support. The results of a two-year evaluation of Barnardo's services providing for sexually exploited children and young people showed a full spectrum of disadvantage experienced by the young people concerned. Of the 42 young people using 10 Barnardo's services, 19 had spent some part of their childhood in the looked-after system, only four had no apparent history of abuse or neglect, almost all had disengaged from school in their early teens, with 63% going missing from home at the initial assessment prior to referral to the project and one-third of this 63% going missing for prolonged periods of time (Scott and Skidmore, 2006: 43). Of a study of 55 young people, the 21 who were persistently selling sex were the most alienated from services, the most difficult to engage and carried the largest number of problems at any one time (Pearce et al, 2003).

Rather than penalising the young person who persistently returns to selling sex, and perceiving the problem only as a child protection issue precipitated by inadequate parenting and exploitative individuals, we need to move away from the legacy of the Victorian era and move into the 21st century with a strand of policy for sexually exploited children and young people that actively supports youth service and outreach interventions, accompanied by distance-learning materials and specific benefits that address the impact of poverty. This cannot be delivered by child protection services alone. They need support from trained and specialist youth workers, education workers and targeted independent-living and employment schemes.

To move forward in this way should be possible. Referring to recent developments in central government, there has been a considerable drive to address child poverty and the disadvantage that accompanies it (HM Government, 2008a). In 1999 the government made a pledge to end child poverty within a generation – by 2020. The first target, to lift one million children out of poverty, was missed by 300,000. To meet the 2010 target, the number of children in poverty must fall to 1.7 million. It is currently at 2.9 million (before housing costs) (HM Treasury, 2008). Indeed, the Treasury noted that:

> Many people believe there is very little child poverty in the UK today. This is not the case: over a fifth of children are in poverty. The Government believes it is one of the most corrosive social issues facing the country, and it touches each and every person, indirectly if not directly. Child poverty is everyone's problem, and tackling it needs to be everyone's business. (HM Treasury, 2008: 6)

And:

> Local authorities have a critical role in helping to eradicate child poverty by leading local action, engaging with and harnessing the resources of local communities to increase employment opportunities for all, preventing those at risk from falling into poverty and improving the life chances of young people. (HM Treasury, 2008: 3)

The *Every Child Matters* agenda (HM Government, 2003) clearly states five outcomes for young people that each local authority children's trust should deliver, one of them being to keep young people safe. The subsequent *Staying safe: Action plan* (HM Government, 2008b) identifies sexual exploitation as a significant threat to young people's well-being, to be addressed through implementation of the preventative initiatives proposed in the prostitution strategy (Home Office, 2006) and through the health initiatives advanced in the cross-governmental sexual violence and abuse action plan (HM Government, 2008b). There is no shortage of positive speaking and policy directives from central government as to how poverty and abuse can be addressed. But the question remains: how can these overarching central government initiatives be translated into local interventions that really do impact on sexually exploited young people's lives?

The history of local intervention to challenge sexual exploitation within community settings is poor. A review of a targeted 50 localities showed that although 84% said that they knew of children involved in prostitution in their area, only 14% had made any progress in intervening against the abuse, and only 6% said that they were meeting the dual aim of the *Safeguarding Children Involved in Prostitution* guidance (SCIP guidance) (DH, 2000) of protecting children *and* prosecuting abusers (Swann and Balding, 2002). A more recent scoping exercise sent out requests for information on services for sexually exploited children and young people to the 144 safeguarding children boards in the country. Only 20 responded with positive actions to be included in the scoping exercise, 14 of whom had specific protocols in place to address sexual exploitation (Jago and Pearce, 2008: 10). An audit of services for sexually exploited children and young people identified 41 services in the four jurisdictions of the UK, the vast majority of which were voluntary organisations, often struggling for funding (Phoenix 2002). The government is currently updating the SCIP guidance, suggesting that every local safeguarding children board should have an interagency subcommittee with practitioners dedicated to responding to sexually exploited children and young people's needs and to making resources available to target those most 'at risk' and intervene to support them into education and training. With the renewed focus on sexual exploitation generated through the rewriting of the guidance, we have the opportunity to focus on how this broad government agenda of reducing child poverty, indeed of eliminating child poverty by 2020, and of keeping all young people safe, can be enacted at the local level, to the advantage of sexually exploited children and young people.

To do this I want to identify three areas that make a significant contribution to any young person's successful transition to adulthood: housing; training and employment; and violence and abuse. Without either a safe place to live, a source of income, and freedom from violence young people will be severely disadvantaged in their efforts to gain an independent living. As I have argued above, intervention that is led exclusively through child protection services will concentrate on protecting the vulnerable child from abuse rather than on empowering the developing adult to employ their own agency and seek an independent living.

Housing, training and employment

Studies of sexually exploited children and young people show that access to safe and permanent accommodation is central to their continued desistence from sexual exploitation. A 2003 study of 55 sexually exploited young women showed that 18 were homeless (Pearce et al, 2003). Melrose and Barrett (2004) note studies of sexually exploited young people who were without safe accommodation, running from their family or care home and who were swapping sex for a bed for the night. *A Coordinated Prostitution Strategy* (Home Office, 2006) highlights the problems facing the large number of sexually exploited young people who run from home and go missing, noting that housing agencies 'will be fully involved' in children's trusts (Home Office, 2006: 31). Again, the problem becomes translating this into *local* practice. Research shows that more than one million children in Britain live in housing that is overcrowded, temporary, run down, damp or dangerous (Rice, 2006); that 8.1 million homes in England fail to met the government's decent homes standard (CLG, 2007) and that more than 112,000 homeless children are living in temporary accommodation (CLG, 2008). Poor housing conditions are known to increase the risk of severe ill health and problems at school (Mitchell, 2004; Harker, 2006). Two-thirds of respondents to a Shelter survey among homeless households living in temporary accommodation said that their children had problems at school (Shelter, 2008). However, despite these problems, Shelter is concerned that housing does not feature strongly enough in the *Every Child Matters* agenda and believes that:

> access to decent affordable housing must be at the heart of any strategy for improving the life chances of children and young people and reducing child poverty. (Shelter, 2008: 3)

It advocates that the government issue guidelines to ensure that housing departments and organisations work with other agencies to meet the needs of homeless 16- and 17-year-olds and that peer education is promoted to help prevent continued homelessness among young people. This is particularly the case for sexually exploited children and young people, who often go missing from home, experiment with efforts to establish their own independent accommodation and use peer groups and potentially abusive adults for places to stay. Work to date suggests that 'joined up' approaches between housing, leisure and social work intervention can be successful in supporting these young people (Sheffield Safeguarding Children Board, 2007; Street Reach, 2007). If a foster carer is trained to understand sexual exploitation and is supported by a 'rapid response' team of named practitioners in police, specialist youth services and social work, the young person can be encouraged to develop a relationship with 'home' (Sheffield Safeguarding Children Board, 2008). These interventions do appear to support the young person into independent living if they are able to build a relationship with a foster carer who understands the difficulties facing them and who is, in turn, supported by a dedicated and experienced team of practitioners in containing the anxiety of managing the problematic behaviour. Although this is labour intensive, it means that the young person has been given an opportunity to feel that there is a home that can 'contain' their fluctuating feelings, that can tolerate periods of distress, vulnerability or rebellion, and provide a platform to begin to develop independent living skills.

Similarly, the foyer movement is beginning to work well with some local authorities and housing associations to provide supported independent living programmes for young people (www.foyer.net). The Swan Housing Group, for example, runs foyers for young people aged 16 to 25 which aim to help vulnerable young homeless people gain confidence and reach their full potential. A network of services provides a backup service to the foyers, encouraging the young people to access education and employment possibilities, while simultaneously supporting them to use their key worker in a way that builds positive relationships (Swan Housing Group, 2006/7). Some trained, specialist and supported foster placements do manage to reach out and engage with a sexually exploited young person. However, a 'replacement' home, such as a foster home, is not always applicable for a 16- or 17-year-old who has run from family environments before and who finds it difficult to settle within a family. Some of the initiatives, such as those being developed with foyers, offer an opportunity for a sexually exploited young person to be integrated into group living and independence. The key to both specialist foster care and independent living schemes is that they are supported by named, dedicated staff who understand the dynamics facing the young person and who can provide a rapid response to help both the young person and the foster carer or key worker when needed. This may require intensive input during the initial stages of placement but this will, with time, reduce as the young person settles. More thought, commitment, time and money needs to be given to advancing these schemes if challenging child poverty, keeping young people safe and preventing exploitation is to occur. Direct and targeted funding needs to be placed into these developments to build the interagency work that is proposed under local authority children's trusts. Essentially, for older sexually exploited young people who are approaching school-leaving age and adulthood, these independent living projects need to be supported, as well as interventions that focus on developing statutory child protection services. They cannot function to the advantage of the young person on their own. Housing is one part of the project. Helping the young person to gain access to training and employment is of equal importance.

Training and employment

Central aims within the strategy to reduce child poverty have been to increase the number of young people in employment and to decrease the number of children and young people not in education and training. Research argues that being out of school and employment makes young people particularly vulnerable to sexual exploitation. Those who are known to be exploited are also known to have a history of truanting or of being excluded from school.

Research has also established that being not in education, employment or training (NEET) is linked to a number of other poor outcomes, including low levels of attainment, and higher levels of teenage conception. In 2008, the government figures suggested that the proportion of NEETs has fallen between 2006 (10.4%) and 2007 (9.4%).[1] This is claimed to be due specifically to the developing NEET strategy, which is structured around four themes: careful tracking to identify those at risk; personalised guidance and support; to enable young people to access suitable provision; and to tackle barriers to learning.

While it is commendable that the number of NEETs appears to be reducing, the problem is that those who continue to be out of school, training or employment are the most damaged and challenging young people. Until the NEET strategy is translated into genuine practice in local areas to reach and work with very vulnerable young people, there will continue to be a group that remains isolated. As argued by a Joseph Rowntree Foundation study on poverty and exclusion, the

> Government will need to extend its policy of increasing redistribution to low-income families and long-term

policies working in this direction include better education
and training for disadvantaged groups. (JRF, 2006: 1)

Gaining access to training, and sustaining involvement, will be major
challenges to sexually exploited young people whose peers and abusive
partners may not want them to be part of a training scheme, who may
be struggling to develop a safe and secure home, who may have difficult
memories of education and who may feel depressed and disheartened
about their ability to manage.

One good example of a project intervention that addressed each of
these difficulties is of work of the Street Reach project in Doncaster.
Street Reach runs a distance-learning programme through a partnership
agreement between local schools, youth service and the dedicated sexual
exploitation project, and invites young people to create portfolios for
Duke of Edinburgh Awards. Being given assistance (travel time and
repeated reminders of the venue and purpose of the meeting) young
people are encouraged to attend school-based sessions, youth centre
activities and outreach programmes. They collect data, drawings, activity
charts and personal reviews that contribute to a portfolio of work.
This scheme, labour-intensive in the early stages, builds the young
person's confidence in working with teaching and training staff, builds
their ability to engage with and reflect on learning activities, and has
resulted in many finding work in part-time employment schemes or
jobs within which they can continue their training.

Such schemes demonstrate that solely offering a job or training
scheme to sexually exploited children and young people is not enough.
An intensive pre-employment period is needed where timetables,
time management and engagement in learning relationships are all
supported by a key-worker relationship that is capable of engaging
with counselling and therapeutic intervention. If this support is offered,
the young person can begin to develop the confidence and basic skills
needed to engage with the training and employment agenda (Street
Reach, 2007).

I have argued above that seeing the sexually exploited young person
solely as a victim of abuse in need of child protection is inadequate.
Such young people, particularly those who are over 16, who are able
to consent to sexual relationships and who are seeking independence
in their transition to adulthood, need support through housing and
training initiatives. As research has shown, those young people who are
especially vulnerable to sexual exploitation have experienced poverty
and deprivation. These initiatives, therefore, need to be integrated into
the agenda focused on challenging child poverty. As such, funding,

training and strategic management needs to be directed at a local level to support the targeted activities reaching out into communities and local specialist services supporting sexually exploited young people.

Violence and sexual exploitation

Much has been said above about sexually exploited young people being difficult to engage. Often the young people are intimately involved with cultures of violence, either familial, peer-group and/or sexual violence (Melrose and Barrett, 2006; Scott and Skidmore, 2006). Engaging with violent youth cultures is notoriously hard and, indeed, potentially dangerous for workers who are motivated to help the young people concerned. As Pitts explains, the young people, both young women and young men, may be 'reluctant' recruits in violent gang cultures that allow little scope for escape from the violent culture (Pitts, 2008). The dynamics of sexual exploitation suggest that the young person can quickly be 'trapped' into a violent sexual relationship. Rarely will the offer of an alternative housing placement or the suggestion of a new training scheme make any sense to them unless such offers can also engage with the reality of the impact of violence.

Research has shown that the sexual exploitation of children and young people often (although not always) involves the threat or use of violence. There is invariably a culture of violence surrounding the sexual exploitation of young people and children. As with the experience of young people in gangs, this culture of violence 'normalises' violence for the individual (Pitts, 2008). But in situations of sexual exploitation, the actual violence is at the interpersonal, intimate level. In this way it is similar to the violence experienced by adults in domestic violence situations. Whether or not the sexually exploited young person will perceive themself to be a victim of violence or describe themself in this way is not clear. What is clear is that in order to engage with them, the intimate and interpersonal violence that they are experiencing must be incorporated within the strategy for engagement. Children's services child protection interventions are, in the main, designed to respond to fundamentally different types of violence, that is, violence within the home perpetrated against children by family members. This has not equipped them to understand or to manage the interpersonal domestic violence that sexually exploited children and young people experience with those who are abusing them (Pearce, 2007).

The reasons are threefold. First, access to the young person is different. They will often be 'transient', living either at home, with a 'boyfriend' or with friends and peers who are intimately involved in life-styles where violence is commonplace. 'Rescuing' a young person from this situation is impossible if they do not understand why and how it is in their own interests. With a history of running away from conflict or 'going missing', the young person will 'disappear' from view until the rescue attempt has been thwarted.

Second, as with an adult experiencing domestic violence, the young person may well be in love with their abuser. The young person may not want to leave, may be saying that they are happy and that their situation will improve if they 'stick with it'. We have learned from work on domestic violence that a 'victim' may leave the violent partner, but that this may take considerable time. It may take repeated attempts for the person to leave the violent situation, and leaving might only occur after a trusting relationship has been built with project workers who are able to offer secure and safe alternative accommodation (Women's Aid, 2006). This leads to the third reason why supporting a young person to leave a sexually exploitative relationship cannot be done through statutory child protection teams alone. For the young person to leave an exploitative situation, they need to be offered a better alternative, as they may say that they have little else in their lives at the time, other than the abusive relationship.

Conclusion

To challenge the young person's view that they have to remain 'stuck' in a violent, exploitative relationship, child protection interventions must be accompanied by employment and housing schemes similar to those noted above. This means education services, employment and training services, housing and youth services working together to offer targeted and sustained support to young people. This support will need to recognise that the young person may leave and then return to violent relationship(s), may start, move away from and restart a training course, may engage with a worker and then try to destroy the relationship because a good relationship is too threatening and unfamiliar to be tolerated. The dynamics that take place in accessing and engaging with sexually exploited young people who are in abusive relationships are complex. They cannot be addressed through simplistic visions of the young person as a vulnerable victim waiting to be rescued from abuse. To change this, the locus of intervention needs to develop from one orientated solely around child protection, to multiple loci that include mainstream social welfare agencies. It is only through broadening the scope of intervention that it will be possible to create an approach to sexually exploited children and young people that advances their sense of agency and works with the highly complex, victimising and undermining nature of their lived experiences. As noted in the introduction to this chapter, each and every one of us responds to difficult situations in different ways. To support a young person to understand and challenge the situations that they face, we will need integrated, supported and targeted approaches involving the range of services that include education, housing and training. The existing good practice that has been developed through the child protection and safeguarding children agenda needs to extend so as to develop a coordinated approach with a range of other services to challenge the sexual exploitation of children and young people. An essential component in this must be to address the impact of poverty and social exclusion on young people's lives, and to work with them to offer scope for change.

Note

[1] www.everychildmatters.gov.uk/neetstrategy

EIGHT

From 'toleration' to zero tolerance: a view from the ground in Scotland

Ruth Morgan Thomas

Introduction

In an ideal world the need for individuals to sell or buy sexual services *in order to survive* would not exist; every citizen of the world would be able to achieve both economic security and sexual fulfilment without recourse to selling or buying sex. The root causes of many – but not all – individuals' entry into the sex industry, such as debt and poverty, gender inequality and gender politics, lack of economic opportunity, low educational attainment, childhood neglect and abuse, and drug dependency would have been eradicated. However, we are a long way away from such a society, and policy should be rooted in the real world, ensuring that no one pays the price for ideological aspirations that cannot be met in the immediate future. Sex workers should not be seen as expendable for political goals.

In 1992, Edinburgh launched its zero tolerance campaign towards violence against women, in which the city committed itself to proactively addressing the issue of violence against women. It should be proud that it was the first city in the United Kingdom to introduce a crime prevention campaign relating to gender-based violence. But some time prior to this Edinburgh had adopted equally progressive approaches to other social issues. In the 1980s, Edinburgh responded strategically to the increased recognition of violence against sex workers and the emerging HIV epidemic. The city developed, through partnership with the City of Edinburgh Council, Lothian and Borders Police, Lothian Health Board and community-based organisations, what became known in the media as a 'tolerance zone' for street prostitution and a pragmatic, complaint-led approach to indoor prostitution. This was in operation for almost 20 years. It was introduced following the brutal murder of two women and escalating crime associated with street prostitution, and was reinforced with the emergence of the HIV epidemic among injecting drug users in Edinburgh and the need to provide accessible harm-reduction services. Within the designated area, women were not charged for soliciting or loitering for the purposes of prostitution – but other illegal activities were *never* ignored. The strategy developed over time – in the early 1990s Lothian and Borders Police appointed the first police liaison officer for sex workers, who took on a welfare rather than an enforcement role, and instead of the police imposing rules for the designated area, ground rules were reviewed, negotiated and agreed between the police and the women. It was not a desolate area that was ignored by the police, nor one in which drug dealers, 'pimps', partners, or child abuse through prostitution were tolerated. It was a primarily non-residential area in which agencies provided accessible services and police worked with the women to ensure that criminality was minimised and that women were protected. A multi-disciplinary partnership between sex workers, the police, the local authority, the NHS and voluntary organisations (including SCOT-PEP, the Scottish Prostitutes Education Project[1]) developed, enabling the targeting of support and services, which brought about real and tangible benefits. Edinburgh should be proud that it prioritised the safety, health, and well-being of women involved in prostitution.

However, nearly two decades have elapsed and we are a long way away from those pioneering days of tackling actual violence and the vulnerabilities of those selling sex in Scotland. The politics of prostitution have intervened and policy making in Scotland has become informed by ideology with little or a disputed evidence base – with the result that sex workers, unlike other communities of interest, have been excluded as irrelevant in informing policy developments that have dramatically shaped their well-being and will continue to do so in the future. In the present climate, 'zero tolerance' has come to mean something very different from the tolerant approach of the 1980s and 1990s. Now, 'zero tolerance' in the context of sex work means recriminalising sex workers and their clients and creating policies aimed at eliminating prostitution – all in the name of protecting women from the assumed violence that prostitution is inherently seen as being.

I have been involved in the sex industry now for more than 28 years – eight years as a sex worker in Edinburgh, two years as an academic researcher at the University of Edinburgh, and 20 years developing services and advocating for sex workers' human, civil and labour rights locally, nationally and globally. Like many sex workers and others, I reject any analysis that defines all prostitution as inherently violence against women, requiring zero tolerance and the eradication of prostitution as a primary goal rather than focusing on addressing the issues which lead people to enter sex work and protecting those engaging in it.

In this chapter I put forward a sex workers' rights perspective in relation to the notion of 'zero tolerance' of prostitution. The rest of the chapter records some of the experiences and voices of sex workers; and presents some of the evidence that calls into question the 'zero tolerance' approach. This evidence was gathered over the last two decades by SCOT-PEP, a community-based organisation that was set up by sex workers for sex workers in 1989 in Edinburgh and which I currently manage.

My main argument is that zero tolerance, in the context of violence against women and sex work, has become dogmatic and unresponsive to the *actual needs* of sex workers. It operates at a number of levels to increase the vulnerability of those involved in selling sex. At a conceptual level it confuses violence experienced by women with consensual sex between adults. The approach cannot acknowledge and address the disproportionate levels of actual violence and hate crimes experienced by sex workers – focusing as it does on the supposed 'violence' of the consensual exchange of sex for money. It alienates and further marginalises those who sell sex, and in particular brands women who choose to sell sex as colluding with male violence and therefore of no significance. It denies women's autonomy and agency, treating those who sell sex as 'legal minors' incapable of making their own decisions about their own lives and defining them as victims needing to be 'rescued' from abuse or 'saved' from themselves. In short, it silences the voices of sex workers and undermines fundamental human rights.

Zero tolerance of domestic violence and prostitution: two separate agendas

When the extent of domestic abuse became widely recognised society did not adopt an abolitionist or zero tolerance policy towards relationships or the institution of marriage – unlike what is currently happening in Scotland. Instead, the focus was to combat the abuse and violence within relationships and reduce individuals' vulnerability to such abuse, through seeking to create environments in which such abuse and violence would not be tolerated by our society, together with the provision of support services for those affected, in line with their self-identified needs and aspirations. Out of the domestic abuse movement developed a strong political message, exemplified in the 'Bill of Rights for Women' adopted by Women's Aid Federation (UK):

> I have the right not to be abused
> I have the right to express anger over past beatings
> I have the right to change the situations
> I have the right to freedom from fear of abuse
> I have the right to request and expect assistance from Police and Social agencies
> I have the right to want a better role model of communications for my children
> I have the right to be treated like an adult
> I have the right to leave the abusive environment
> I have the right to privacy
> I have the right to develop my individual talents and abilities
> I have the right to legally prosecute the abusing spouse
> I have the right not to be perfect
> (www.womens-aid.org.uk/bill_of_rights.php)

At the risk of repetition, zero tolerance of domestic violence did not equate to the condemnation of marriage or relationships. Instead, it became a focus for thinking about and providing services to *improve* women's rights and lives. A Bill of Rights such as this is surely applicable for all sex workers, regardless of gender.

This is not to say that the problems highlighted by the zero-tolerance approach in the context of sex work – alienation, exploitation, abuse, violence and coercion – do not exist in the sex industry. But, as in many other industries, they do not define those selling sex or the sex industry. Similarly, the abuse and violence that is domestic violence do not define women in relationships or the institution of marriage. Any discourse that defines sex work as violence is a simplistic approach that denies the diversity and experiences of sex workers. Such a differentiated approach taken by proponents of zero tolerance in the context of sex work undermines the autonomy and right to self-determination of sex workers that would never be considered appropriate in other arenas. Rejected by advocates of zero tolerance is any notion that sex work is labour. Acceptance of the view that sex work is labour does not mean that the real and tragic harms that can occur within the sex industry should be ignored – it means that we focus on the *actual* violence, abuse and exploitation that sex workers and those coerced or trafficked into the sex industry experience, and we seek to eradicate *these* rather than to eradicate sex work.

Sex work in Scotland – some of the realities

SCOT-PEP estimates there are 800 to 1,000 women selling sexual services in Edinburgh and 3,000 to 5,000 in Scotland every year. The UK Network of Sex Work Projects estimates there are between 50,000 and 80,000 women selling sexual services across the United Kingdom every year. The prostitution mapping undertaken across the United Kingdom in 2006 as part of TAMPEP activities[2] funded by the European Commission estimated that 28% of women (14,000 to 22,400) work in street prostitution while the remaining 72% (36,000 to 57,600) work in indoor establishments and as escorts (TAMPEP, 2004). Medical Research Council research undertaken in 1999 in Edinburgh, Glasgow and Leeds indicated that 81% of street-based sex workers had experienced violence from clients, while 48% of indoor-based sex workers had experienced violence. Only 44% of street-based and 18% of indoor-based sex workers reported an incident to the police (Church et al, 2001).

Violence is actually perpetrated by a small percentage of clients, but, as can be seen from the figures below, the experience of crimes of violence against women selling sex is disproportionate to that experienced by women who are not sex workers, and men appear to seek sex workers out as targets. As Church et al write:

> Despite a growing literature on the prevalence of client violence against prostitutes, little is known of the violent events, how they impact upon women and how and why they occur. Analysing in depth interviews (n=90), we examined women's definitions of client violence constructing a typology of 'bad dates, violent clients and murderous men'. This encompassed the continuum of violence experienced including verbal abuse, hate mail, disrespectful behaviour, rough sex, robbery and serious physical and sexual assault. Critically, social stigma against prostitutes acted to compound the harm women experienced from clients and to encourage client violence. Men's comments and actions during the assaults suggested that many felt justified in behaving viciously and felt that they were outside the reach of the law.
>
> Further, we examined 135 cases of client violence to investigate the nature of the assaults. Contrary to belief that assaults may be 'triggered' due to tensions within the prostitute–client encounter, many attacks were premeditated,

> men often had weapons and even utilised their knowledge
> of the scripts of prostitute encounters to trap women and
> act violently towards them. (Church et al, 2001: 524)

However, the almost exclusive focus on eliminating sex for sale means that 'zero tolerance' of sex work does not allow for campaigns to be initiated that target client violence or that seek to change clients' and society's attitudes towards sex workers other than portraying them as helpless victims. When the media reported the sex workers' rights movement's International Day to End Violence Against Sex Workers following the murder of five women in Ipswich in 2006, the advocates of zero tolerance responded by saying it should be renamed as the International Day to Encourage Violence Against Sex Workers.[3]

What zero tolerance does not see – sex for sale

The key assumption of zero tolerance in the context of sex work is that the commercial exchange of sex for money *is* violence against women. The approach, however, fails to give equal priority to keeping safe those women who decide to continue selling sex and those who are unable to find means of sufficient alternative income generation, as it does to providing routes out of prostitution. It assumes that no woman would choose to sell sex, that every sex worker wants to leave prostitution and that they are able to do so. It ignores the complex issues within the reality of the current world economic order, which is driven by profit and exploitation, and by the feminisation of both poverty and migration. It denies that women decide to sell sexual services for economic reasons relating to financial aspirations as well as survival. It ignores the reality that, if sex work were not an option, many women would have no means of surviving or supporting their families, nor the possibility of achieving their aspirations of financial security for their futures. In its insistence that sex work is violence, it fails to ensure that the fundamental issues that lead to individuals selling sex are addressed.

The zero-tolerance approach to sex work does not allow politicians, policy makers and service providers to improve the conditions within the sex industry, and proponents of zero tolerance in Scotland have said, when giving evidence to the Scottish Parliament, that the more dangerous sex work is, the fewer women will be prepared to sell sex. However, all instances of zero tolerance of prostitution have failed to eradicate the sex industry, even in countries where the selling of sex is a capital offence and women have been publicly put to death. More important, it has failed to protect the very individuals it claims to be seeking to 'rescue'. The fundamental problem for the zero-tolerance approach is that, contrary to its assumptions, the realities are that selling and buying sexual services cannot be isolated from the sexual and the economic spheres or the multiple ways in which they intersect, nor can sex work be separated from human sexuality, with all its diversity. But more than this, sex work cannot simply be dismissed from or ignored within a labour- or income-generation framework, when so many earn their living by sex work.

What zero tolerance cannot see – women who choose not to conform to a 'real woman' role

I made an informed decision to use both my body and my mind as economic resources in choosing to enter sex work and earn money. I did not choose to work in the sex industry because I enjoyed the sex or was ignorant of the risks and dangers involved, but because it was a way of earning the money my family and I needed. I was not forced to work in the sex industry any more than any one of us is forced to find a means of supporting ourselves and achieving our financial aspirations in life.

I did not sell my body – I sold sexual services. The fact that sex becomes work does not remove an individual's right to have control over who they have sex with *or* the sexual services they provide *or* the conditions under which they provide those services. Nor does it mean that violence becomes just part of the job – offering sexual services, whether for payment or pleasure, is not an invitation to any kind of violence. I did not give up or have taken away my right to say NO – I asserted my right to say YES! Sex work is, by definition, consensual sex. I agreed to provide the sexual services to my clients, and on occasions refused clients or declined to provide the services requested. I negotiated the fee for the sexual services to be provided, and declined to provide services if my fee was not met. I negotiated the conditions under which I provided sexual services – including venue, safe sex practices and other intimate details – and refused to provide services outside my own guidelines. As a sex worker, I negotiated and maintained control over the sex I had, far more so than in my non-paying sexual relationships. I was fortunate in this – *but not unique.* I struggle to understand why all feminists are not demanding that all sex workers, and all women, have the right to control the sex they have and the conditions under which they have it – rather than asserting that women should not have the right to have sex if they are to be paid for it, or, worse, infantilising the women involved in sex work and defining it as paid or compensated rape.

I was intrigued when, at a Forum on Discrimination meeting in Glasgow, I met a Muslim woman who was surprised at the similarity of our experience of lack of toleration – a sex worker and a woman who chooses to follow Islam and wear a headscarf. It appeared to both of us that some feminists who are proponents of zero tolerance have very particular ideas about how women should behave and what they should believe and that they have the right to impose their views on all women, either by denying our existence or by questioning our ability to understand the world around us. They seek to educate those of us who do not conform to their views about the wrongness of our ways. These women are rapidly joining the patriarchal moralists in seeking to impose upon women what they can and cannot do with their bodies and, if we fail to fall into line, exclude us from having fundamental human rights. As a feminist myself, my response has not changed – 'My body is my business'. These words are being echoed around the world by thousands of sex workers and yet we seem to be invisible to the advocates of zero tolerance, politicians and policy makers.

What zero tolerance denies – sex workers' rights

Zero tolerance lobbyists, and some policy makers who seek to eradicate prostitution as a social and/or moral evil, argue that sex workers who wish to defend their human rights should not be listened to; or that their motives should be seen as tainted; or that their opinions are ill informed and biased. Those on the extreme are arguing that sex workers should not have the right to organise or even associate, as, according to them, this *fundamental human right* is seen as normalising prostitution, which should not be permitted.

However, all individuals, including female, male and transgender sex workers who decide to enter sex work, and those trafficked and coerced into the sex industry, have the same entitlement under international human rights treaties.[4] Consensual engagement in sex work is the exercise of an individual's human right to choose her or his own occupation. Non-consensual engagement in sex work is forced labour or slavery and sexual violence; it is a gross violation of human rights. Sex workers' rights advocates do not condone such violations – the sex workers' rights movement is about defending the human rights of sex workers and striving to ensure that human rights are respected within the sex industry.

Box 8.1: What are rights?

What are rights?

Rights are freedoms that individuals have in order that they are able to live well and in harmony within society.

Rights are opportunities that citizens are accorded by the support and cooperation of their government.

Rights come with freedom

This means that people will not be prevented by society from exercising their rights. For instance freedom to choose a religion, freedom to information e.g. news, freedom to choose where to live, freedom to travel, and the opportunity to choose your own occupation.

Rights come with responsibilities

Individuals have a responsibility to protect their own rights and the rights of others. Individuals must not infringe on the rights of others in society.

Source: I have Rights, a manual about rights and social equality, produced by Empower Foundation in Thailand for service employees in the sex industry, funded by the ILO (International Labour Organisation). The manual was one of three created by a group of service employees that formed to discuss everyday problems and help develop solutions. Also consulted in drafting the manual were friends, people with knowledge of the situation, and information drawn from written resources and research papers.

Sex workers' loving relationships are often condemned, as though they are not worthy of being loved. While some sex workers are in abusive relationships, all are capable human beings, worthy of being loved and who have the ability to love and to care for other human beings – as any human being.

The lack of recognition of sex work as labour and the criminalisation of activities within and around the sex industry result in sex workers being perceived and treated like criminals, even if they do not break any laws. The stigma imposed on sex workers goes beyond the recognition that they sell sex to earn money. It defines them as intrinsically unworthy and a threat to moral, public and social order, labelling them sinners, criminals, or victims – and separates them from the 'good' and 'decent' citizens within society. It is essential that the human rights of sex workers are recognised and respected. Sex workers should not be perceived purely as victims to be assisted, criminals to be arrested or targets for public health interventions. They should be considered as citizens, with needs and aspirations, who have the potential to make a real contribution to their communities – and who have the right to self-determine what is best for them.

To define sex workers as victims and to seek to eradicate the sex industry through legislation violates the right to work and to free choice of employment and ignores the diverse voices of those selling sexual services. Paradoxically, zero tolerance against sex work actually increases the alienation and vulnerability of those selling and buying sex and provides greater possibilities for abuse, coercion and exploitation within the sex industry by denying labour and fundamental human rights to sex workers.

Sex workers speak out

Increasing numbers of sex workers from all over the world and all sectors of the sex industry are speaking out about the choices they have made in entering the sex industry and their right to equal protection under human and labour rights legislation. Within the European context, the International Committee on the Rights of Sex Workers in Europe has published the *Sex Workers in Europe Manifesto*,[5] which was a collaborative effort between 120 sex workers from 26 European countries and was presented to the European Parliament.[6] At the closing ceremony of the 15th International Aids Conference, Bangkok, in 2004, a poem written by sex workers was read by Pornpit Puckmai from Empower Foundation:

> When I can work in safe and fair conditions.
> When I am free of discrimination.
> When I am free of labels like 'immoral' or 'victim'.
> When I am free from unethical researchers.
> When I am free to do my job without harassment, violence or breaking the law.
> When sex work is recognized as work.
> When we have safety, unity, respect and our rights.
> When I am free to choose my own way.
> THEN I am free to protect myself and others from HIV.

The following year, on International Women's Day, the National Human Rights Commission of Thailand awarded the first annual human rights award for defending the rights of women to Pornpit.

Thirty-six human rights defenders were nominated for the award. The judges' decision was based on the history of the human rights work done by the nominees and they saw Pornpit's work on the promotion of the rights of sex workers as outstanding and most deserving of this award. On receiving the award, Pornpit sent out this message to sex workers around the world:

> I want this award to be an inspiration to all of us sex workers fighting for our rights. I want to say to you that if you are a sex worker and you're thinking about whether to join the fight for sex worker rights then ... do it! I thought that our fight would take 150 years or more but now I'm not so sure we will have to wait that long. It is a huge step that the National Human Rights Commission here in Thailand has given its inaugural award to me, a sex worker who works for the rights of sex workers. This is recognition for all sex workers that we have rights and that we are more than capable of defending our rights. This is not just my award. This is our award. The Power We Have: The Power We Share!

Closer to home, research indicated how beneficial sex workers across Scotland thought that a tolerance zone had been and could be:

> To date, the issue of how prostitution should be regulated (indeed, even whether it should be regulated by the state) has been a debate shaped more by political viewpoints than scientific evidence.... The research ... sought to flesh out women's views ... All of the women interviewed ... supported the idea of a tolerance zone where they could work without fear of arrest and prosecution. Many of the women cited the positive impact on their safety as the main reason for that support. (McKeganey, 2006: 152)

McKeganey interviewed 33 women across the four main Scottish cities. It is worth quoting some of the participants' responses to the question of whether there should be tolerance zones:

> Yes, I think it makes it safer for us ... You would feel a lot safer coming out at night if there are cameras about and there is less chance of you being taken away. (Glasgow)

We need somewhere safer to work because we're spread everywhere we're not in just one area. Everybody's everywhere, and if they gave us a place where we could work it would be a lot safer for all of us. We could all watch each other. (Edinburgh)

... the first thing is that people doing this need safety and a tolerance zone ... the men are scared they think there would be too much emphasis on them driving about so maybe they'll be a bit put off but the women know there is a zone specifically used for prostitution I think it's a good idea. (Aberdeen)

It does help because in my opinion if you've got a problem like a couple of weeks ago a girl we know got raped and before that a girl got attacked and the CID came round and you can really tell them anything. They do help you as much as possible, for instance this little Indian guy took my own knife to ma throat grabbed the phone off me standing on ma hands and that I got it off him and I went up to the normal police upon Union Street but they didn't want to know but when I was down here and the liaison woman came down ... They were a lot more interested. (Aberdeen)

The main benefit is the fact that the lassies stick to the main area. When we were in Coburg Street we stuck to the area we were supposed to be in, right ... When the tolerance zone broke up the lassies stopped looking out for one another. Like at one time lassies would take registrations numbers but you don't do anything like that anymore they don't bother their arses anymore. (Edinburgh)

It would make it safer for us to know who the clients were because sometimes we approach people who aren't looking for business like yourself. (Glasgow)

I think it should be legal, yes, if they were to say walk up and down this street it would be OK because there are no houses here and when you think about it what on earth are we doing wrong to be honest. (Dundee)

> The attitude of the coppers has changed now ... I got attacked about three months ago and I reported it and the coppers made out it was my fault. A guy pulled a knife on me and gave me a few punches. (Edinburgh)

Claims by zero-tolerance advocates that women selling sex on the streets will support 'tolerance zones' *simply* because it will 'make their lives easier' ignore the actual violence experienced by women and do not respect the women's ability to articulate their own needs or understand their own lives and the reality of their current circumstances and the lack of realistic alternatives open to them.

McKeganey's research echoed the evidence provided by SCOT-PEP on behalf of the women working in Edinburgh to the Scottish Parliament and the Scottish Executive since the issue was first raised in Parliament in 2002 by Margo Macdonald MSP, who has fought tirelessly to try to ensure that street-based sex workers are given protection within society (Scottish Executive, 2004). However, Scottish politicians and policy makers in the Scottish Executive have chosen to ignore the voices and experience of women who work in street prostitution and have blindly followed those advocating zero tolerance of prostitution. As time went on, however, the Scottish Parliament chose to ignore not only the voices of sex workers calling for safer working environments but also the recommendations of their own Expert Group on Prostitution, whose report specifically advised the Scottish Executive not to criminalise kerb crawling, on the grounds that the evidence from other countries suggests that such legislation increases violence against an already vulnerable group of women. In February 2007 the Scottish Parliament, following prolonged lobbying by zero-tolerance advocates, passed the Prostitution (Public Places) (Scotland) Act criminalising kerb crawling and the clients of street-based sex workers; the Act came into force on 15 October 2007.

In 2006 the Scottish Executive had defined *all* prostitution as violence against women. It did so without undertaking either the second phase of the Expert Group on Prostitution's review of prostitution policy and legislation, which was scheduled to look at indoor sex work, or the third phase, which was scheduled to look at male sex work, *and* without any consultation with women or men selling sex, or their clients.

SCOT-PEP believed it was important that women whose lives were being defined by government should have an opportunity to have their voices heard. A consultation was undertaken with indoor-based sex workers, who are rarely consulted, around whether they related to the 'violence against women' perspective and how they felt about their involvement in sex work. Thirty-three women took part. Below are some of the responses given to SCOT-PEP.

> I think it depends on if the woman chose to do this or not! If she never then yes, of course it is.

> I do not feel this way, or that the sex industry is about the exploitation of women. I do however feel that certain customers, for example those who are very rough, seek out submissive girls, or who have rape/violent fantasies that they want to role-play do attempt to use prostitutes as a means to try to inflict violence upon women.

> As with any sexual assault or domestic violence case that is not related to prostitution, it's the violence, abuse and exploitation that matters, not the presence of a financial transaction. The essence of the victim's experience is power misuse, whether money is involved or not. Prostitution is simply one possible vehicle for it or context for it. In itself, it is not inherently abusive or unjust.

> I feel fine about it. I chose to do this job and I choose to continue doing it. I don't get any sexual gratification from it, but I don't hate it. I see it as providing a service. Some customers can be very nice, and others not so nice, but this is true of any job which involves dealing with the public. Some days it is very easy money and others you have to work really hard for it, but it is a lot of money for something which is easy to do. I have never felt exploited by any customer or boss, I always use protection, and I don't feel bad about being in this industry.

> I am proud that I am a strong enough person to be able to do this job and not take drugs or drink and I have not let it change me. I am thankful for the experience because I have learned so much, yet it saddens me that it is still not accepted in society so I live a double life. I don't understand why? Society [frowns] upon women like myself who made the choice to do this for a while to better my future and we don't harm anyone.

I work entirely on my own terms, independently after having started in well-run Sydney brothels. Working has always been completely my own decision. This may have a bearing on the experiences I've had. I've always preserved my own boundaries and never done anything I'm not comfortable with, preferring to lose money than be ill treated or feel dehumanised or degraded. I also had a strong clear sense of myself and my own assertiveness before I started working at the age of 26. So, in many ways, I may not be typical but I've also been able to sustain this job for 20 years and enjoyed nearly all of it. I expect the balance of good and bad experiences with clients or colleagues has been roughly the same as in mainstream jobs I've done. I've never been bullied (but my only experience of workplace bullying was in the voluntary sector, ironically, and other instances of exploitation have also happened in the mainstream commercial sector). So overall, my experiences in the sex industry have been better than average.

The Scottish Strategic Framework on Violence Against Women, produced by the Violence Against Women Team, defined all sex work, from pole-dancing through to prostitution, as violence against women, regardless of what individual women may say about their sex work (Scottish Executive, 2006). They did so without consultation with either the women in the sex industry or the GMB union, which represents the interests of sex workers through its Adult Entertainment branch.

While violence is never acceptable, equally it should never be acceptable for policy makers to ignore their responsibilities to consult with key stakeholders or for them to dismiss so easily the views of women whose lives they impact upon. Sex workers are more than aware of the potential for violence, abuse and exploitation within their industry; they do not ignore the real harm that some experience. However, the stories of horror and abuse do not define every sex worker's experience, nor do the stories of success and empowerment. Prostitution is not inherently violent and abusive; nor is it inherently empowering. The potential for violence and exploitation can be reduced and the potential for empowerment increased if government works *with* the experts – sex workers. We are part of the solution, not part of the problem.

Two decades of listening, talking, watching and learning together

There are those who seem to believe that prostitution cannot and should not be managed; however, Edinburgh's experience from the 1980s and 1990s shows that the adoption of a pragmatic, non-judgemental approach towards prostitution can provide undeniable benefits to sex workers, their clients and the community at large. The loss of that approach to street prostitution, coinciding with World AIDS Day 2001, has shown how easily those benefits can be lost and the high price sex workers have to pay for a zero-tolerance approach to prostitution.

Getting it right for sex workers

SCOT-PEP estimates that the introduction of a designated area for street prostitution, alongside the emergence of both licensed and unlicensed establishments and the use of the internet in Edinburgh, has resulted in 85% of Edinburgh's female sex workers working indoors in a *safer* environment than that faced by women working on the streets. While the remainder of this chapter will focus on the impact of having a designated area and the changes experienced by street-based sex workers when a zero-tolerance approach was introduced in Edinburgh, it is important not to forget or ignore the situation of indoor-based sex workers particularly with the increased police initiatives across the United Kingdom.

In contrast to the information put out by zero-tolerance advocates about 'toleration zones', street prostitution in Edinburgh decreased during the period in which toleration zones were in operation. The number of local women selling sex on the streets was estimated to be 200 in the early 1980s.[7] In 2000, SCOT-PEP estimated that this number fell to fewer than 150 women – unlike in other cities across the United Kingdom, where many sex-work projects reported street prostitution increasing significantly. It was also one of the safest cities in the UK for street-based sex workers during the operation of the 'toleration zone'.

However, the benefits did attract women from outside the city of Edinburgh; in the last two years of operation more than 50% of women working within the designated area came from other parts of Scotland, primarily the west coast and Glasgow. SCOT-PEP statistics for 2000 show that more than 10% of the 1,400 women estimated to be selling sex on the streets of Glasgow at some point travelled to Edinburgh to work in that year, doubling the number of women selling sex on the streets of Edinburgh. The reasons given by women were that Glasgow operated a zero-tolerance policy and Edinburgh was safer, not only in terms of not being charged by the police but also in relation to their personal safety, *and* they could earn more money per client in Edinburgh. Given that the vast majority of the women travelling from Glasgow were chaotic, dependent drug users, the fact that they were prepared to take the time and effort and pay drivers £40 or more to bring them through to Edinburgh to work speaks volumes.

The operation of the designated area was not without its problems – but women worked collectively and looked out for one another, the benefits of which can be measured against the patterns that have emerged since a zero-tolerance approach was introduced in Edinburgh at the end of 2001. By 2002 women selling sex on the streets of Edinburgh were regularly being cautioned and charged. In July 2004 the City of Edinburgh Council initiated legal proceedings to obtain Anti-Social Behaviour Orders against street-based sex workers and in February 2007 the clients of street-based sex workers were criminalised.

Violence against sex workers

In 2001, with 218 women working on the streets, there were 11 incidents reported to SCOT-PEP by street-based sex workers, 73% (8) of which were reported to the police. When the designated area was abandoned in December 2001, women who had previously come to Edinburgh from the west coast of Scotland to work returned to work in Glasgow (a city in which seven women had been murdered in the previous decade), as they reported that it felt safer, in terms of both violence from clients and prosecution. In 2003, with 150 women working on the streets, there were 111 incidents reported, 5% (6) of which were reported to the police. In the two years following the loss of the designated area, SCOT-PEP witnessed a 1000% increase in attacks against the women. In 2007, with 100 women working on the streets, there were 126 incidents reported to SCOT-PEP.

While zero tolerance may be seen to reduce the numbers of women selling sex on our streets, it is also evident that it significantly increases the violence experienced by women who remain with no viable alternatives and by those who continue to enter street prostitution. The cooperation and trust between the women and the police, established during the operation of a designated area, deteriorates: women no longer see the police as their protectors, but rather as their persecutors.

New Futures and moving on

In 1999, SCOT-PEP established a New Futures project, to enable those wishing to look at alternatives to explore their options and to support them in achieving their goals. During the 2½ years of the project 96 individuals (approximately 10% of the sex workers accessing SCOT-PEP) accessed support. At the end of the project in March 2002, 80% of the individuals who had participated were no longer active in the Edinburgh sex industry (Table 8.1).

Table 8.1: SCOT-PEP New Futures project statistics

	Service users	New service users	Repeat service users	Moved on*
2000	61	61	0	
2001–02	67	35	32	29 (48%)
2002–03	project closed	0	19	48 (72%)
Total	**96**			**77 (80%)**

* Moving on is defined as not in contact with SCOT-PEP and therefore probably not working in Edinburgh's sex industry.

Its success rate was higher among indoor-based sex workers (Table 8.2) than among street-based sex workers (Table 8.3), as there was no integration with or fast-track access from the New Futures project to drug treatment services. SCOT-PEP has been tracking mobility into and out of the sex industry in Edinburgh since 2000. Its statistics show that the majority of women who sell sexual services in Edinburgh are involved on a short-term or intermittent basis.

The statistics show that women selling sex on the streets of Edinburgh are becoming more entrenched as the zero-tolerance approach impacts on the street prostitution scene, this despite the increase in services from partner agencies to support them moving on. The acute deterioration of the working environment for women selling sex on the streets of Edinburgh has not prevented new women from entering street prostitution. SCOT-PEP recorded nine new service users through street outreach services in the first quarter of 2008.

It follows that with such a mobile population of street and indoor-based sex workers, harm reduction must remain a priority within service provision requirements to protect the health and safety of sex workers and their clients, and thereby the community at large.

Table 8.2: SCOT-PEP moving on statistics for indoor-based sex workers

	Service users	New service users	Repeat service users (from previous year)	Moved on
2000	327	236	91	141 (61%)
2001–02	402	254	148	179 (55%)
2002–03	358	219	139	263 (65%)
2003–04	317	127	190	168 (47%)
2004–05	292	112	149	168 (53%)
2005–06	303	152	151	141 (48%)
2006–07	360	199	161	142 (47%)
2007–08	320	146	174	186 (52%)

Table 8.3: SCOT-PEP moving on statistics for street-based sex workers

	Service users	New service users	Repeat service users (from previous year)	Moved on
2000	287	176	111	145 (57%)
2001–02*	234	116	118	169 (59%)
2002–03	126	62	64	170 (73%)†
2003–04	130	52	78	48 (38%)‡
2004–05	93	44	49	81 (62%)
2005–06	87	37	50	43 (46%)
2006–07	89	31	58	29 (33%)
2007–08	94	29	65	24 (27%)

*This covers a 15-month time period.

† This increase represents both the outcome of the New Futures Project and the fact that women from the west coast of Scotland stopped coming to Edinburgh to work. Sixty-five (57%) of local women moved on during the period of monitoring.

‡ The introduction of ASBOs in Edinburgh had a significant impact: approximately 10% of local women started to travel to work in Glasgow, which did not impose ASBOs, and to Aberdeen, in particular, as it operated a 'tolerance zone'.

Accessibility of services

In 2001 97% (212/218) of street-based service users accessed the services in the drop-in which was located on the edge of the designated area. At that point, with drop-in and street outreach services running five nights a week, SCOT-PEP was confident that it was reaching 95% of women selling sex on the streets of Edinburgh. In 2003–04, with drop-in and outreach services reduced to two nights a week, due to loss of funding, the ongoing dispersal of street prostitution across two to three square miles of residential and non-residential streets in North Leith and the introduction of ASBOs, only 65% (97/150) of street-based service users accessed the services in the mobile drop-in.

In the last quarter of 2007, following the introduction of the 2007 Prostitution (Public Places) (Scotland) Act and the resultant police initiatives against clients, SCOT-PEP has witnessed the further displacement of street-based sex workers – geographically, temporally and to other sex-work settings and criminal activities. SCOT-PEP statistics show a 27% decrease in the number of contacts, although there was only a 15% decrease in the number of individuals seen. SCOT-PEP has received numerous reports, from regular service users, of women working on nights and at times when services are not available, or changing their means of contacting clients, making it almost impossible to establish direct contact and provide support. As the zero-tolerance approach encroaches further onto the street prostitution scene it has become increasingly difficult to locate and identify women selling sex on the streets of Edinburgh. It would be dangerous for anyone to assume that such figures represent a real and long-term decrease in the number of women selling sex, rather than a temporary or permanent reconfiguration of selling sex in public places.

It is essential, if society is to succeed in reducing the vulnerability of street-based sex workers, that support services be able to establish contact with them and for them to feel confident in being able to access support services. Zero tolerance drives sex workers into inaccessible methods of working, drives them away from the possibility of receiving support that will enable them to choose their own route, which for many will – if all their needs are addressed – mean moving on from sex work.

Criminality within the street prostitution scene

During the operation of the designated area in Edinburgh the presence of drug dealers, 'pimps' and 'minders' was minimised through police management and control of the designated area. Women selling sex, including drug users, reported the presence of undesirables to SCOT-PEP or directly to the police – and these individuals were rapidly dealt with.

In 2001 fewer than 50% of the local women selling sex were doing so primarily as a result of drug dependency, in contrast to women from

Glasgow, among whom drug dependency was higher than 95%. While there was a 35% (40) decrease in the number of local women selling sex on the streets between 2001 and 2004, drug dependency among the women rose to more than 95%, with 70% injecting.

As street prostitution dispersed, drug dealers moved in and started targeting the women. In 2003 SCOT-PEP reported a new trend emerging in Edinburgh: that of 'drug pimping', whereby women who had built up debts with dealers were encouraged, and on occasions coerced, into street prostitution as a means of paying off their debt and continuing their supply. Partners and minders who had previously not been tolerated within the designated area became visible as women sought ways of trying to protect themselves from the increasing levels of violence and harassment. This abuse came not only from clients, but from local residents seeking to drive the women out of the area and members of the general public who came to the area specifically to abuse and throw missiles at the women for 'fun'. In addition, women increasingly became the victims of robbery and extortion as criminals saw them as easy targets who were unlikely to go to the police.

Zero tolerance has removed the police force's ability to effectively manage and control the situation, despite ongoing high levels of police activity.

Community safety and collective working and lessons from Scotland

Since 2001 Lothian and Borders Police have been proactively policing street prostitution – cautioning and charging women with loitering and soliciting. The number of visible women selling sex on the streets may have diminished, but street prostitution has not disappeared. The women have dispersed to avoid the attention of law enforcement and residents. Street prostitution now covers two to three square miles of both residential and non-residential streets across North Leith, with an average of only 10 women spread over that area each night – rather than the 250 yards of non-residential street in the designated area where women worked within sight of one another. Collective working, which kept women safer, is history. Women no longer work in pairs or take registration numbers and look out for one another – they are too busy trying to survive in a hostile environment. *The street prostitution scene in Edinburgh is radically different.*

Sex workers have paid a heavy price for the loss of Edinburgh's pragmatic, non-judgemental approach – which operated within a human rights framework and focused on the empowerment of sex workers. The evidence would indicate that it was essential to harm reduction for sex workers and in sex-work settings, but it was equally important for the prevention of involuntary sex work and providing effective support to enable sex workers who wished to move on from sex work to do so. It is time to move beyond tolerance and compassion and recognise the value and rights of each and every individual — including those who choose to sell sex and those who choose to buy sex.

Notes

[1] SCOT-PEP is registered as a Scottish charity: Scottish Charity Number SC020657. For further information see www.scot-pep.org.uk

[2] A pan-European network of sex-work projects working with migrant and mobile female and transgender sex workers in the field of HIV prevention and human rights. The mapping was to be repeated in 2008; www.tampep.com

[3] This view was expressed in a letter to *The Herald* following an opinion article that was supportive of the International Day to End Violence Against Sex Workers. See 'The buying of sex cannot be tolerated', *The Herald*, 22 February 2008.

[4] See Declaration of the Rights of Sex Workers in Europe: www.sexworkeurope. org/site/index.php?option=com_content&task=view&id=35&Itemid=199

[5] www.sexworkeurope.org/site/index.php?option=com_content&task=vie w&id=24&Itemid=189

[6] See www.sexworkeurope.org for more information.

[7] Estimate provided in Written Submission by DCC Tom Wood, Lothian and Borders Police, to Local Government Committee, Scottish Parliament, December 2002, www.scottish.parliament.uk/business/committees/historic/ x-lg/papers-02/lgp02–33.pdf

NINE

Conclusion

Jo Phoenix

A number of dominant themes arise in this book. Each of the chapters has sought to analyse specific aspects of the UK's emerging prostitution policy and has done this through using both empirical and theoretical research. All of the authors have posed questions about how particular categories of individuals are constructed within the key documents that have shaped and given rise to the policies now in place and the legislation being proposed. Similarly, all of the authors have called into question not only the assumptions underpinning these documents and policies, but also the myths and misconceptions about what individuals in the sex industry 'need' or 'want'. Taken together, these chapters provide a damning critique of New Labour's 'coherent' strategy on prostitution, and especially on the abolitionist objective and the strategy of 'enforcement plus support', in which welfare interventions are placed alongside criminal justice mechanisms. The chapters also challenge a number of all-too-easy assumptions:

- that sex work somehow threatens community cohesion, safety and security;
- that forcing drug-using sex workers to seek treatment for their drug use and misuse will lever them out of prostitution;
- that men in sex work can (or should) be treated like women in sex work; and
- that child protection methods of work are most appropriate for sexually exploited children and young people.

Notwithstanding the specific critiques contained in each chapter, as a whole this volume raises a number of questions on prostitution policy and its reform more generally. This chapter addresses some of these wider questions.

The battle over meanings

First among these wider questions is the question of how to critique or engage with policy in a field where the key signifier (that is, prostitution) is one which is both highly contested and, as argued in the Introduction, capable of signifying almost any type of social anxiety about sex, danger, violence and community destruction. One of the dominant themes running throughout the book is the dispute over meaning that is taking place between the individuals living with or engaging in prostitution (including sex workers, non-governmental organisation workers, local community members and residents of areas with a street-based sex-work scene), central government, academics and campaigners. Of course, this is not new. Contestation and challenge over the meanings of sex work have occurred for at least two millennia.

So it should come as no surprise to the informed reader that most of the contributors begin by challenging the meanings that New Labour has ascribed to 'sex work' and 'sex workers' – and in particular calling into question the related assumptions that: sex work is violence; sex workers (as adults, as men, as women, as young people) are victims; and 'communities' want redress from the nuisance, threat and danger of prostitution. For instance, Pearce's chapter on children and young people begins with the assertion that while it makes a type of 'common sense' for government to assume that sexually exploited children and young people are child victims of sexually abusive or exploitative men, to base policy on such an assumption belies the complex social and material realities of young people's lives in the UK today. Similarly, O'Neill's and Melrose's contributions remind readers that while many individuals in sex work experience violent victimisation, they are not always and already 'victims', any more than their experiences in sex work can be reduced to being merely and only a manifestation of violence. Morgan Thomas's chapter tackles this question directly. She shows the reader how a policy based on the rhetoric of 'zero tolerance' towards violence against women so easily becomes a platform from which sex workers' rights can be curtailed and services for them be withdrawn. Whowell and Gaffney's chapter likewise starts with the assumption that not only do the experiences of men who sell sex differ from women, but also sex work comes to take on fundamentally different meanings for men than for women – especially in relation to gay culture and identities. Scoular et al's chapter, just as O'Neill's, also provides strong empirical evidence to argue that individuals in local communities that have a street-based sex-work scene are not always and already threatened by that sex work nor, indeed, intolerant towards individual sex workers.

That said, both those chapters also point to the frustrations that local residents felt towards the local authorities in not addressing their *complex* concerns about street-based sex work – concerns that are not reducible to a simple desire to move sex work out of *their* neighbourhoods.

Whatever the specific claims about 'the problem' of prostitution are, this volume attests to the way in which this 'battle over meanings' tells the reader as much about current social, political, ideological and economic concerns as it does about prostitution itself. So for instance, as suggested by Scoular et al, many of the local residents and community members' concerns about prostitution had as much to do with urban decline as the local authorities' concerns had to do with urban regeneration. The 'battle' over the meaning of prostitution, in that instance, may not be a contest about the truth of prostitution at all. Pearce's chapter provides an insight into how central government constructs, frames and regulates childhood and youth. More particularly, it generates insights into the assumptions made by New Labour about its role in shaping the young lives of its citizens. What is occluded from present policy discourse on prostitution is the recognition that the lives of young people in 21st-century Britain *can* be so violently shattered by the effects of poverty, familial breakdown, education exclusion and violence and abuse that selling sex for money *can* be understood by those young people as either preferable to other alternatives or, indeed, a way to fashion a better life for themselves in the future. Whowell and Gaffney's analysis of the contest of meanings suggests that there is a creeping re-regulation of some aspects of gay culture.

As I suggested in the opening chapter, constitutive of the discourse on prostitution is a process of metonymy, and this is reflected in each of the chapters in the book. In their individual ways, they have all argued that one of the key problems in current attempts to create a 'coherent' policy on prostitution in the UK is precisely that the policy process has become a 'renaming game' which privileges particular ideologies of prostitution (as community threat, as gendered violence) and in so doing acts to exclude other understandings, voices and experiences of sex workers, of drug users, of community residents, of male sex workers, of young people or, indeed, of empowered, fully conscious and rational economic agents in a sexual marketplace. Furthermore, taken together, the chapters indicate that now (just as in the late Victorian era) the discourse of prostitution can be and is strategically deployed in the service of shifting modes of and challenges to governance (of and in local communities, of drug users, of gay men, of young people).

Whatever the specific nature of the contest of meanings may be, this volume also highlights an important issue for academics and researchers, policy makers and campaigners. The *actual* interventions proposed by the policy reform process treat sex work, sex workers, residents and all the other actors in the field as epiphenomenal to the various social anxieties that have prompted the reforms. In such a context, it may well be that the most appropriate political point of intervention is not necessarily challenging the constructions of prostitution that underpin the policy process, but rather highlighting and bringing to the fore the grounded empirical realities that tend to become obscured, including the effects of poverty, victimisation, violence and social exclusion on the lives of many sex workers, both in relation to their sex work and, importantly, outside it.

'Evidence'-based policy reform? The exclusion of alternative voices and research

The second dominant theme that arises from this volume is the question of 'evidence'. What counted as evidence in the prostitution policy reform? Whose voices and views were included? Whose were excluded? This question is not unique to prostitution policy reform. It has been a question or theme in critical engagement with New Labour's policy making for a number of years – especially in relation to criminal justice policy.

When newly elected in 1997, New Labour promised to 'modernise' government. 'Evidence-based policy' was hailed as being one of the key strategies by which modernisation could occur, through the way it radically reconceived the relationship between knowledge production, policy and practice. New Labour claimed to be a 'thinking government' in which policy would be based on evidence of 'what works' and not on political ideologies and dogma. The *Modernising Government* White Paper (Cabinet Office, 1999) put forward this 'new' formula for policy making:

> Policy decisions should be based on sound evidence. The raw ingredient of evidence is information. Good quality policy making depends on high quality information, derived from a variety of sources – expert knowledge; existing domestic and international research; existing statistics; stakeholder consultation; evaluation of previous policies ... (Cabinet Office, 1999: 31)

Such was the centrality of this formula that when addressing the main independent funding organisation of social research in the UK, the

Economic and Social Research Council, the then Home Secretary, David Blunkett, declaimed:

> This Government has given a clear commitment that we will be guided not by dogma but by an open-minded approach to understanding what works and why. This is central to our agenda for modernising government: using information and knowledge much more effectively and creatively at the heart of policy making and policy delivery. (David Blunkett, speech to the ESRC, 2 February 2002)

Notwithstanding the tremendous growth in government research into many aspects of social policy that occurred over the last decade, Hillyard et al (2004) argue that New Labour's hunger for 'evidence' and 'research', especially in regard to crime and justice, has been highly partial and selective. As they note in a carefully detailed article on the relationship between criminological knowledge production and the state, policies on, *inter alia*, corporate killing and deaths in the workplace have not been subject to the same type of scrutiny as more conventional 'justice' interventions. Their argument is that the expansion of 'research' on crime and criminal justice matters has been utilitarian, in that it serves to maintain and legitimate particular definitions of 'the problem' that must be addressed. Central to this argument is that not only are particular issues left out, but government research agendas are almost entirely focused on 'evaluating' their own interventions. In relation to prisons, Carlen (2002) argued that this 'research' is problematic: that it is not framed by or carried out with the same type of intellectual rigour, social understandings, theoretical frameworks or methodological demands of 'proper' social research; that evaluation research has become an industry *which generates its own demand and then supplies it*; and, more importantly, that 'what works' research, by definition, cannot challenge its own terms of reference.

Prostitution policy reform has not been untouched by this process. As each of the chapters in this volume shows, the 'evidence' and 'research' that were deployed in the consultation document *Paying the Price* (Home Office, 2004) and in the final published *Coordinated Prostitution Strategy* (Home Office, 2006) was highly selective, partial and, most importantly, legitimated the abolitionist direction as well as the 'enforcement plus support' strategy. Sanders' chapter addresses this issue by detailing the manner in which the consultation document neglected to mention models of regulating indoor sex work that are generally thought of as successful (that is, Las Vegas, in Nevada, and

Germany) while simultaneously describing only the limitations of the Australian and Austrian models. O'Neill's chapter provides a detailed description of the manner in which the voices and experiences of sex workers are mis-recognised, marginalised and excluded in the policy process. Scoular et al's chapter demonstrates how the policy reform process effectively silenced and excluded the tolerant voices from communities which have a street-based sex-work scene, just as Melrose's chapter demonstrates the exclusion of credible research about the nature of drug addiction. Of course, the main argument of Whowell and Gaffney's chapter was precisely that the policy reform process had silenced the views and experiences of male sex workers almost completely, just as Pearce's chapter implied that the views and experiences of young people that did not accord with stereotypes and ideologies of victimhood were silenced. Morgan Thomas's chapter demonstrates how the alternative discourse of sex workers' rights was theoretically silenced by the power and dominance of a discourse of prostitution as violence. Just as important, Morgan Thomas's chapter also demonstrates how local proponents of the 'zero tolerance' approach in Edinburgh suppressed women's actual views and acted to disqualify the experiences of project workers and sex workers in Scotland. Morgan Thomas describes how the Scottish Executive concluded in 2006 that *all* prostitution was violence against women, despite the fact that it had not completed the second or third phase of its own review process, and without consulting any individuals in the sex industry. Morgan Thomas's chapter also repeats the claims made in Sanders' chapter, that in Scotland, just as in England and Wales, indoor workers have not been consulted *at all*, and nor have any of the trade unions which support the work of sex workers, such as the GMB (Britain's general union).

It is possible to make three related claims based on the contents of this volume. First, the chapters all demonstrate that the 'evidence' that has been cited and used in the consultation documents and the process of policy reform is highly selective. Second, what has been hailed as evidence is the polemical and rhetorical claims which decontextualise it, and not the voices from those involved in prostitution (either as residents, sex workers, project workers or trade union representatives), nor the decades of research which make the claim that prostitution cannot be understood outside a socio-economic context. Third, the process of reforming the UK's prostitution policy at the beginning of the 21st century has amounted to little more than the ideological legitimation of an abolitionist stance on selling sex.

The role of the projects: the death of the 'non-judgemental' non-governmental sex-work project

The final theme to arise from this volume is the question of the relationship between 'policy' or 'regulation' and 'the problem' of prostitution. Many of the chapters argued that the reforms to policy will have (or are having) adverse consequences on specific populations of those involved in selling sex for money. Pearce described the anomalous 'persistent returners' clause that permits the full range of criminal justice disposals to be used against sexually exploited children and young people if they are assessed as voluntarily engaging in prostitution. Most of the chapters describe the increased levels of regulation and criminalisation that specific populations of sex workers are now facing. Similarly, they all describe the deleterious effect of an 'enforcement plus support' approach wherein actual interventions in sex workers' lives (and the sex industry) are achieved through a combination of criminal justice measures, which are used to encourage individuals into welfare services in order that those welfare services can provide the support deemed necessary to enable the sex workers to quit sex work. Melrose's chapter on drug interventions eloquently describes some of the paradoxical, perverse and contradictory effects of pursuing such a policy in regard to drug-using sex workers.

Melrose's chapter also raises a central issue, which is also echoed by each of the contributors, about the relationship between governmental and non-governmental welfare- (or harm reduction) orientated agencies working with those involved in prostitution, and the new forms of regulation and governance of sex work. One of the consequences of the change in direction of prostitution policy, towards abolitionism, is that previously autonomous organisations are now being pulled closer into 'partnership' working with statutory criminal justice agencies. Although this has been happening in regard to general drug treatment programmes, in relation to sex work this shift in working relationships is new and can potentially have devastating impacts on the projects working with sex workers and on the funding arrangements for those projects. The projects themselves are not unaware of this. As shown in Scoular et al's chapter, there is scepticism from project workers about the nature and direction of reforms to prostitution policy in the UK. Not only do the data Scoular et al present demonstrate that the projects question the long-term benefits of the enforcement-plus-support approach, they also question whether the policy shift has been made because it is a less expensive option than dealing with the myriad problems that many sex workers have. But I wish to draw out one of the implications of the data and arguments presented in this volume. Previously many of the projects working with individuals in the sex industry have been successful for a number of related reasons. They offer a non-judgemental service that deals with the individual's difficulties. The funding that they have attracted has often been received from the Department of Health (not the Home Office) and with the remit to increase individuals' sexual health and reduce the spread and risk of sexually transmitted diseases. This has meant that projects have been able to offer confidential services and to work autonomously of the more coercive state agencies of criminal justice. But with New Labour's policy shift towards abolitionism and away from harm reduction the ability of these agencies to continue to offer autonomous, non-judgemental interventions is being called into question. As Whowell and Gaffney's chapter attests, funding from either the Department of Health or the Home Office is increasingly tied to the demands that projects work with criminal justice agencies and have an explicit aim of exiting sex workers from prostitution. It is too early to determine what consequences this has had on the nature and effect of provision for sex workers, but the early signs are that projects will find themselves experiencing increasing difficulties in providing non-judgemental services – something that arguably will mean that sex workers face increased risks of violence, ill health and difficulties in accessing other social and personal services, such as housing or social welfare benefits. For instance, SCOT-PEP in Edinburgh had to cease providing outreach and support services for sex workers in 2009, after 20 years of service provision, because the local health authority reduced its funding by two-thirds. This means that there is now no dedicated service for sex workers in Edinburgh. It is not possible to say that this was a direct result of the abolitionist policy shift in Scotland, but it coincides with it, and given that SCOT-PEP continued to challenge the direction of policy and argue for a non-judgemental approach, it is most likely attributable, at least in part, to the declared aim of the Scottish Executive to have 'zero tolerance' towards sex work.

Conclusion

It is difficult to overestimate the potentially profound effects that will be felt by sex workers and sex-work projects from the move towards an abolitionist policy on prostitution in the UK. As mentioned in the Introduction, in two subsequent years there have been two attempts to criminalise the purchase of sex in the UK, despite the evidence from Sweden that such moves reduce neither prostitution nor the difficulties of violence and exploitation associated with it. Long-standing sex-work projects are either closing or reporting difficulties in funding. The use of criminal justice measures against women in prostitution (in particular Anti-Social Behaviour Orders) is on the rise. In addition, there are current proposals before parliament to create compulsory rehabilitation orders to be used against individuals to compel them to seek help to leave prostitution. All of this is happening at a time when the UK is experiencing recession and perhaps moving into one of the worst economic depressions of recent times – with all the attendant increases in unemployment and poverty. If the social research into sex work has indicated anything, it has indicated that selling sex is one of the various strategies women deploy when faced with few other realistic economic choices. Research has also indicated that women, particularly those who are single or are lone parents, are most at risk of poverty. It is these women who are most likely to experience the worst effects of Britain's declining economic environment. While there may well have been a general decrease in the numbers of women in sex work in the last decade (see Matthews, 2008) – or at least in the more visible street-based sex work – this trend could well be reversed in the next few years as more women move into poverty. Just at a time when more and more individual sex workers may be in need of non-judgemental personal welfare services, it would appear that the UK is opting to deal with the problems of prostitution through compelling them onto programmes of exit. The questions then arise: how will these women resource themselves in non-criminogenic ways? As this volume attests, the future of provision and policy for sex workers and sexually exploited children and young people seems to be a future shaped by salvationism backed by the coercive arm of criminal justice sanctions. As was ever the case, those hit the hardest by these new ways of regulating selling sex in the UK are likely to be those women, men and young people whose involvement in prostitution is driven by poverty and economic necessity.

References

Abbot, S.A. (2000) 'Motivations for pursuing an acting career in pornography', in R. Weitzer (ed) *Sex for sale: Prostitution, pornography and the sex industry*, London: Routledge.

Aggleton, P. (ed) (1999) *Men who sell sex: International perspectives on male prostitution and HIV/AIDS*, Philadelphia: Temple University Press.

Agustin, L.M. (2006) 'The conundrum of women's agency: migrations and the sex industry', in R. Campbell and M. O'Neill (eds) *Sex work now*, Cullompton: Willan Publishing.

Agustin, L.M. (2007) *Sex at the margins: Migration, labour markets and the rescue industry*, London: Zed Books.

Allen, D.M. (1980) 'Young male prostitutes: a psychosocial study', *Archives of Sexual Behaviour*, vol 9, no 5, pp 399–426.

Arendt, H. (1970) *On violence*, New York: Harcourt Brace and Co.

Aris, R. and Pitcher, J. (2004) *Evaluation of Coventry SWISH arrest referral scheme for sex workers: Final report*, London: Terrence Higgins Trust.

Atkins, M. (2007) 'Objects that look: how is ambiguity of body and self maintained in the public sex encounter?', unpublished MA thesis, Manchester: Manchester University.

Attwood, F. (2006) 'Sexed up: theorizing the sexualization of culture', *Sexualities*, vol 9, no 1, pp 7–94.

Barnard, M. (1993) 'Violence and vulnerability: conditions for street working prostitutes', *Sociology of Health & Illness*, vol 15, no 5, pp 683–705.

Barton, A. (1999) 'Sentenced to treatment? Criminal justice orders and the health service', *Critical Social Policy*, vol 19, no 4, pp 463–84.

BBC (2006) 'Oaten resigns over rent boy claim', http://news.bbc.co.uk/1/hi/uk_politics/4635916.stm, accessed 15 August 2008.

Bell, D. (2001) 'Fragments for a queer city', in D. Bell, J. Binnie, R. Holliday, R. Longhurst and R. Peace (eds) *Pleasure zones: Bodies, cities, spaces*, New York: Syracuse Press.

Bellamy, K., Bennett, F. and Millar, J. (2006) *Who benefits? A gendered analysis of the UK benefits and tax credits system*, London: Fawcett Society.

Bernstein, E. (2001) 'The meaning of the purchase: desire, demand and the commerce of sex', *Ethnography*, vol 2, no 3, pp 389–420.

Bernstein, E. (2007) 'Sex work for the middle classes', *Sexualities*, vol 10, no 4, pp 473–88.

Bimbi, D. (2007) 'Male prostitution: pathology, paradigms and progress', *Journal of Homosexuality*, vol 53, no 1, pp 7–35.

Bindman, J. and Doezema, J. (1997) *Redefining prostitution as sex work on the international agenda*, www.walnet.org/csis/papers/redefining. html#1

Bland, L. (1982) '"Guardians of the Race" or "Vampires on the Nation's Health"?' in E. Whitelegg (ed) *The Changing Experience of Women*, London: Martin Robinson.

Bloor, M.J., McKeganey, N.P. and Barnard, M.A. (1990) 'An ethnographic study of HIV-related risk practices among Glasgow rent boys and their clients', *AIDS Care*, vol 1, no 1, pp 17–24.

Bourgois, P. (1996) *In search of respect: Selling crack in El Barrio*, Cambridge: Cambridge University Press.

Boynton, P. and Cusick, L. (2006) 'Sex workers to pay the price', *British Medical Journal*, vol 332, 28 January, pp 190–1.

Brents, B. and Hausbeck, K. (2005) 'Violence and legalized brothel prostitution in Nevada: examining safety, risk and prostitution policy', *Journal of Interpersonal Violence*, vol 20, no 3, pp 270–95.

Brooks-Gordon, B. (2005) 'Clients and commercial sex: reflections on Paying the Price: a consultation paper on prostitution', *Criminal Law Review*, June, pp 425–43.

Brooks-Gordon, B. (2006) *The price of sex: Prostitution, policy and society*, Cullompton: Willan Publishing.

Brown, S. (1998) *Understanding youth crime*, Buckingham: Open University Press.

Buchanan, J. (2004) 'Missing links? Problem drug use and social exclusion', *Probation Journal*, vol 51, no 4, pp 387–97.

Cabinet Office (1999) *Modernising Government*, Cm 4310, London: The Stationery Office.

Campbell, N. (2000) *Using women: Gender, drug policy and social justice*, New York: Routledge.

Campbell, R. and Farley, M. (2006) *Towards a strategy on sex work for Brighton and Hove: Service monitoring and sex worker views and experiences*, Brighton & Hove: Brighton & Hove City Council, Sex Work Strategy Group.

Campbell, R. and Hancock, L. (1998) 'Sex work in the climate of zero tolerance: hearing loud voices and the silence of dissent', Paper presented at Sex Work Reassessed, University of East London, 9 September.

Carlen, P. (2002) 'Carceral clawback: the case of women's imprisonment in Canada', *Punishment & Society*, vol 4, issue 1, pp 115–21.

Carnwath, T. and Smith, I. (2002) *Heroin century*, London: Routledge.

Chapkis, W. (2003) 'Trafficking, migration, and the law: protecting innocents, punishing immigrants', *Gender & Society*, vol 17, no 6, pp 923–37.

Church, S., Henderson, M., Barnard, M. and Hart, G. (2001) 'Violence by clients towards female prostitutes in different work settings: questionnaire survey', *British Medical Journal*, no 322, pp 524–5.

Clarke, J. (2004) 'Dissolving the public realm? The logics and limits of neo-liberalism', *Journal of Social Policy* vol 33, no 1, pp 27–48.

Clarke, J. and Newman, J. (1997) *The managerial state: Power, politics and ideology in the remaking of social welfare*, Thousand Oaks, CA: Sage.

CLG (Department for Communities and Local Government) (2007) *English House Condition Survey headline report 2006*, London: CLG.

CLG (2008) *Statutory homelessness statistics*, London: CLG (March).

Cohen, S. (1972) *Folk devils and moral panics: The creation of Mods and Rockers*, London: MacGibbon and Kee.

Coleman, J. and Scofield, J. (2007) *Key Data on Adolescence*, 6th edn, Brighton: Trust for the Study of Adolescence.

Connell, J. and Hart, G. (2003) 'An overview of male sex work in Edinburgh and Glasgow: the male sex worker perspective', Occasional Paper 8, Glasgow: Medical Research Council, Social and Public Health Sciences Unit.

Correlation Network (2008) *Practical guideline to providing health services to sex workers*, Netherlands: DHV-AMOC.

Coy, M (2006) 'This morning I'm a researcher, this afternoon I'm an outreach worker: ethical dilemmas in practitioner research' in *International Journal of Social Research Methodology* vol 9, no 5, pp 419–31.

Craine, S. (1997) 'The black magic roundabout: cyclical transitions, social exclusion and alternative careers', in R. MacDonald (ed) *Youth, 'the underclass' and social exclusion*, London: Routledge.

Crawford, A. (1997) *The local governance of crime: Appeals to community and partnerships*, Oxford: Clarendon.

Criminal Law Revision Committee (1985) *17th Report: Prostitution: off-street activities*, Cmnd 9213, London: The Stationery Office.

Crosby, S. and Barrett, D. (1997) 'Poverty, drugs and youth prostitution: a case study', in A. Marlow and G. Pearson (eds) *Young people, drugs and community safety*, Lyme Regis: Russell House Publishing.

Cull, M., Platzer, H. and Balloch, S. (2006) *Out on my own: Understanding the experiences and needs of homeless lesbian, gay, bisexual and transgender youth*, Brighton: University of Brighton, Faculty of Health and Social Policy Research Centre.

Cusick, L. and Berney, L. (2005) 'Prioritizing punitive responses over public health: commentary on the Home Office consultation document Paying the Price', *Critical Social Policy*, vol 25, no 4, pp 596–606.

Cusick, L., Martin, A. and May, T. (2003) *Vulnerability and involvement in drug use and sex*, London: Home Office Research, Development and Statistics Directorate.

Davis, P. and Feldman, R. (1991) *Male sex workers in South Wales*, Project Sigma Working Papers, Southbank University, London: HMSO.

Davis, P. and Feldman, R. (1997) 'Prostitute men now', in G. Scambler and A. Scambler (eds) *Re-thinking prostitution: Purchasing sex in the 1990s*, London: Routledge.

DCSF (Department for Children, Schools and Families) (2008) *Draft re-write of the SCIP guidance: Safeguarding sexually exploited children and young people*, London: The Stationery Office.

Dean, H. and Melrose, M. (1997) 'Manageable discord: fraud and resistance in the social security system', *Social Policy and Administration*, vol 3, no 2, pp 103–18.

Dean, H. and Melrose, M. (1999) 'Easy pickings or hard profession? Begging as an economic activity', in H. Dean (ed) *Begging questions: Street level economic activity and social policy failure*, Bristol: The Policy Press.

Deisher, R.W., Eisner, V. and Sulzbacher, S.I. (1969) 'The young male prostitute', *Paediatrics*, vol 43, no 6, pp 936–41.

DH (Department of Health)/HO(Home Office) (2000) *Safeguarding children involved in prostitution*, London: HMSO.

Dorais, M. (2003) *Rent boys: The world of male sex trade workers*, Quebec: McGill-Queens University Press.

Eaton, M. (1993) *Women after prison*, Milton Keynes: Open University Press.

Edwards, S. (1993) 'Selling the body, keeping the soul: sexuality, power and the theories and realities of prostitution', in S. Scott and D. Morgan (eds) *Body matters: Essays on the sociology of the body*, London: Falmer Press.

Edwards, S. (1997) 'The legal regulation of prostitution: a human rights issue', in G. Scambler and A. Scambler (eds) *Rethinking prostitution: Purchasing sex in the 1990s*, London: Routledge.

Ekberg, G. (2004) 'The Swedish law that prohibits the purchase of sexual services: best practices for prevention of prostitution and trafficking in human beings', *Violence Against Women*, vol 10, no 10, pp 1187–218.

Ericksson, J. (2005) 'The Swedish model: arguments and consequences', presented to Prostitution in Europa – Nationale Gesetze und europapolitische Perspektiven, Feministisches Institut der Heinrich-Böll-Stiftung, Berlin, 16 March.

European Commission (2006) *Gender inequalities in the risks of poverty and social exclusion for disadvantages groups in thirty European countries*, European Commission, Directorate-General for Employment, Social Affairs and Equal Opportunities, Luxemburg.

European Commission (2008) *Report on equality between men and women*, European Commission, Directorate-General for Employment, Social Affairs and Equal Opportunities, Luxemburg.

Faugier, J. and Sargeant, M. (1997) 'Boyfriends, "pimps" and clients', in G. Scambler and A. Scambler (eds) *Rethinking prostitution: Purchasing sex in the 1990s*, London: Routledge.

FitzGerald, M. (2001) 'Ethnic minorities and community safety', in R. Matthews and J. Pitts (eds) *Crime, disorder and community safety*, London: Routledge.

Fraser, N. (1995) 'From redistribution to recognition? Dilemmas of justice in a post-socialist age', *New Left Review*, vol a, pp 68–93.

Fraser, N. (2000) 'Rethinking recognition', in *New Left Review*, May/June, pp 107–20.

Gaffney, J. (2002) 'Guidelines for development of outreach work with men who sell sex', in K. Schiffer (ed) *Manual: Tips, tricks and models of good practice for service providers considering, planning or implementing services for male sex workers*, Amsterdam: European Network Male Prostitution.

Gaffney, J. and Beverley, K. (2001) 'Contextualising the construction and social organisation of the commercial male sex industry in London at the beginning of the 21st century', *Feminist Review*, vol 67, no 1, pp 133–41.

Gamble, A. (2000) 'Economic governance', in J. Pierre (ed) *Debating governance: Authority, steering and demoncracy*, Oxford: Oxford University Press.

Garland, D. (1997) 'Governmentality and the problem of crime: Foucault, criminology, sociology', *Theoretical Criminology*, vol 2, pp 173–214.

Garland, D. (2001) *The culture of control: Crime and social order in contemporary society*, Oxford: Oxford University Press.

Gil-Robles, A. (2004) *Report by Mr Alvaro Gil-Robles, Commissioner for Human Rights, on his visit to the United Kingdom*, 4–12 November 2004, CommDH (2005) 6, Strasbourg: Office for the Commissioner on Human Rights.

Gorham, D. (1978) 'The "maiden tribute of modern Babylon" re-examined: child prostitution and the idea of childhood in late-Victorian England', *Victorian Studies*, vol 21, no 3 pp 353–79.

Hancock, L. (2006) 'Community safety and social exclusion', in P. Squires (ed) *Community safety: Critical perspectives on policy and practice*, Bristol: The Policy Press.

Hanmer, J. and Saunders, S. (1984) *Well-founded fear: A community study of violence to women*, London: Hutchinson.

Hanmer J., Radford, J. and Stanko, E. (eds) (1989) *Women, policing and male violence: International perspectives*, London: Routledge.

Harcourt, C. and Donovan, B. (2005) 'The many faces of sex work', *Sexually Transmitted Infections*, vol 81, no 3, pp 201–6.

Harding, T. (2006) 'Gender, drugs and policy', in R. Hughes, R. Lart and P. Higate (eds) *Drugs: Policy and politics*, Berkshire: Open University Press.

Harker, L. (2006) *Chance of a lifetime: The impact of bad housing on children's lives*, London: Shelter.

Harris, M. (1973) *The Dilly Boys: The game of male prostitution in Piccadilly*, London: Croom Helm.

Harris, P. (2006) *Drug induced*, Lyme Regis: Russell House Publishing.

Hester, M. and Westmarland, N. (2004) *Tackling street prostitution: Towards an holistic approach*, Home Office Research Study 279, London: The Stationery Office.

Hickson, F., Weatherburn, P., Hows, J. and Davis, P. (1994) 'Selling safer sex: male masseurs and escorts in the UK', in P. Aggleton, P. Davies and G. Hart (eds) *AIDS: Foundations for the future*, London: Taylor & Francis.

Hill, M. (1990) 'The manifest and latent lessons of *child abuse enquiries*', *British Journal of Social Work*, pp 197–213.

Hillyard, P., Sim, J., Tombs, S. and Whyte, D. (2004) 'Leaving a stain upon the silence: contemporary criminology and the politics of dissent', *British Journal of Criminology*, vol 44, no 3, pp 369–90.

HM Government (2003) *Every child matters*, Norwich: The Stationery Office.

HM Government (2008a) *Ending child poverty: Making it happen*, London: HM Treasury.

HM Government (2008b) *Staying safe: Action plan*, London: DCSF/HM Government, http://publications.everychildmatters.gov.uk/eOrderingDownload/DCSF-00151-2008.pdf

HM Treasury (2008) *Ending child poverty: Everybody's business*, London: HM Treasury.

Holden, K. (2006) *In my skin: A memoir*, Edinburgh: Cannongate Books Ltd.

Home Office (2000) *Setting the Boundaries: Reforming the law on sexual offences Parts I & II*, London: The Stationery Office.

Home Office (2002) *Protecting the Public: Strengthening protection against sex offenders and reforming the law on sexual offences*, London: The Stationery Office.

Home Office (2004) *Paying the Price: A consultation paper on prostitution*, London: The Stationery Office, www.homeoffice.gov.uk/documents/ paying_the_price.pdf

Home Office (2006) *A Coordinated Prostitution Strategy and a summary of responses to 'Paying the Price'*, London: Home Office, www.homeoffice. gov.uk/documents/cons-paying-the-price

Hubbard, P. (1998) 'Community action and the displacement of street prostitution: evidence from British cities', *Geoforum*, vol 29, no 3, pp 269–86.

Hubbard, P. (1999) *Sex and the city: Geographies of prostitution in the urban West*, Aldershot: Ashgate.

Hubbard, P. (2004a) 'Cleansing the metropolis: sex work and the politics of zero tolerance', *Urban Studies*, vol 41, no 9, pp 1687–702.

Hubbard, P. (2004b) 'Revenge and injustice in the neoliberal city: uncovering masculinist agendas', *Antipode*, vol 36, no 4, pp 665–86.

Hubbard, P. and Whowell, M. (2008) 'Revisiting the red light district: still neglected, immoral and marginal?', *Geoforum*, vol 39, no 5, pp 1743–55.

Hubbard, P., Campbell, R., Pitcher, J., O'Neill, M. and Scoular, J. (2006) 'An urban renaissance for all?', in R. Atkinson and G. Helms (eds) *Securing an urban renaissance: Crime, community and British urban policy*, Bristol: The Policy Press.

Hudson, P. and Rivers, I. (2002) *Men and boys: Selling sex in the Bradford district*, Social Inclusion Diversity Paper No 1, York: York St John College of the University of Leeds.

Hunter, G. and May, T. (2004) *Solutions and strategies: Drug problems and street sex markets. Guidance for partnerships and providers*, London: Home Office.

Jacobsson, P. (2006) 'The Swedish model', Paper presented to The Ins and Outs of Sex Work and the Law: Exploring the Legal Frameworks in Different Countries conference, City University of Hong Kong, Hong Kong, 22 October.

Jago, S. and Pearce, J. (2008) *Gathering evidence of the sexual exploitation of children and young people: A scoping exercise*, Luton: University of Bedfordshire.

Jeal, N. and Salisbury, C. (2004) 'Self-reported experiences of health services among female street-based prostitutes: a cross-sectional survey', *British Journal of General Practice*, vol 54, no 504, pp 515–19.

Jeal, N. and Salisbury, C. (2007) 'Health needs and service use of parlour-based prostitutes compared with street-based prostitutes: a cross sectional survey', *British Journal of Obstetrics and Gynaecology*, vol 114 (March), pp 875–81.

Jones, H. and Sagar, T. (2001) 'Crime and Disorder Act 1998: prostitution and the anti-social behaviour order', *Criminal Law Review*, pp 873–85.

Jordan, B. (1996) *A theory of poverty and social exclusion*, Cambridge: Polity Press

Jordan, B. (1999) 'Begging: the global context and international comparisons', in H. Dean (ed) *Begging questions: Street level economic activity and social policy failure*, Bristol: The Policy Press.

Jordan, B. and Redley, P. (1994) 'Polarisation, underclass and the welfare state', *Work, Employment and Society*, vol 8, no 2, pp 153–76.

JRF (Joseph Rowntree Foundation) (2006) *What will it take to end child poverty?*, www.jrf.org.uk/child poverty and www.jrf.org.uk/knowledge/findings/buletsearh.asp

Kelly, L. (1988) *Surviving sexual violence*, Cambridge: Polity Press.

Kelly, L. and Regan, L. (2000) *Stopping traffic: Exploring the extent of, and responses to, trafficking in women for sexual exploitation in the UK*, Police Research Paper 125, London: The Stationery Office.

Kempadoo, K. with Sanghera, J. and Pattanaik, B. (eds) (2005) *Trafficking and prostitution reconsidered: New perspectives on migration, sex work and human rights*, London: Paradigm.

Kinnell, H. (2006) 'Murder made easy: the final solution to prostitution', in R. Campbell and M. O'Neill (eds) *Sex work now*, Cullompton: Willan Publishing.

Kohn, M. (2001) *Dope girls*, London: Granta.

Kooiman, J. (1993) *Modern governance: New government–society interactions*, Newbury Park, CA: Sage Publications.

Kulick, D. (in press) 'Brazilian soccer superstar caught playing with too many balls', *Anthropology Now*.

Laclau, E. and Mouffe, C. (2001) *Hegemony and socialist strategy: Towards a radical democratic politics*, London: Verso.

Laskowski, S. (2002) 'The new German Prostitution Act – an important step to a more rational view of prostitution as an ordinary profession in accordance with European Community law', *The International Journal of Comparative Labour Law and Industrial Relations*, vol 18, no 4, pp 479–91.

Lister, R. (2007) 'Social justice: meanings and politics', Public lecture given at Glasgow University, as Donald Dewar Visiting Professor of Social Justice, published as *The scales of social justice*, Scottish Centre for Research on Social Justice, www.scrsj.ac.uk

London Assembly (2005) *Street prostitution in London*, London: Safer London Committee.

Lowman, J. (2000) 'Violence and the outlaw status of (street) prostitution in Canada', *Violence Against Women*, vol 6, no 9, pp 987–1011.

Maher, L. and Curtis, R. (1992) 'Women on the edge of crime: crack-cocaine and the changing context of street-level sex work in New York City', *Crime, Law and Social Change*, vol 18, no 3, pp 221–58.

Malloch, M. (2004) 'Missing out: gender, drugs and justice', *Probation Journal*, vol 51, no 4, pp 295–308.

Matthews, R. (1986) 'Beyond Wolfenden? Prostitution, politics and the law', in R. Matthews and J. Young (eds) *Confronting crime*, London: Sage Publications.

Matthews, R. (1993) *Kerb-crawling, prostitution and multi-agency policing*, Police Research Group Paper No 43, London: The Stationery Office

Matthews, R. (2008) *Prostitution, politics and policy*, Routledge: London.

Matthews, R. and Pitts, J. (2001) 'Introduction: beyond criminology?', in R. Matthews and J. Pitts (eds), *Crime, disorder and community safety*, London: Routledge.

May, T., Haracopos, A. and Turnbull, P. (2001) *Selling sex in the city: An evaluation of a targeted arrest referral scheme for sex workers in Kings Cross*, Social Science Research Papers No 14, London: Criminal Policy Research Unit, South Bank University.

May, T., Edmunds, M., Hough, M. and Harvey, C. (1999) *Street business: The links between sex and drug markets*, Police Research Series Paper 118, London: Home Office.

Mayhew, H. [1967] (1861) *London labour and the London poor*, London: Frank Cass.

McGhee, D. (2006) 'Community safety and lesbian, gay, bisexual and transgender communities', in P. Squires (ed) *Community safety: Critical perspectives on policy and practice*, Bristol: The Policy Press.

McKeganey, N. (2006) 'Street prostitution in Scotland: the views of working women', *Drugs: Education, Prevention and Policy*, vol 13, no 2, pp 151–66.

McKeganey, N. and Barnard, M. (1996) *Sex work on the streets: Prostitutes and their clients*, Buckingham: Open University Press.

McKinney, C. and Gaffney, J. (2000) 'They think of the pleasure, not the risk: male sex workers as health promoters', Presentation at C3: 3rd National CHAPS conference, Manchester, 1 March.

McLeod, E. (1982) *Women working: Prostitution now*, London: Croom Helm.

McNaughton, C. and Sanders, T. (2007) 'Housing and transitional phases out of "disordered" lives: the case of leaving homelessness and street sex work', *Housing Studies*, vol 22, no 6, pp 885–900.

McSweeney, T. and Turnbull, P. (2007) *Exploring user perceptions of occasional and controlled heroin use*, York: Joseph Rowntree Foundation.

Measor, L. and Squires, P. (2000) *Young people and community safety*, Aldershot: Ashgate.

Melrose, M. (2003) 'Street prostitution and community safety: a case of contested meaning?', *Community Safety Journal*, vol 2, no 1, pp 21–31.

Melrose, M. (2005) 'Living in the shadows: street culture and its role in the development and maintenance of survival strategies of socially marginal young people', unpublished PhD thesis, University of Luton.

Melrose, M. (2006a) 'Trying to make a silk purse from a sow's ear? A comment on the government's prostitution strategy', *Community Safety Journal*, vol 5, no 2, pp 4–13.

Melrose, M. (2006b) 'Young people and drugs', in R. Hughes, R. Lart and P. Higate (eds) *Drugs: Policy and politics*, Buckinghamshire: Open University Press.

Melrose, M. (2007) 'The government's new prostitution strategy: a cheap fix for drug using sex workers?' *Community Safety Journal*, vol 6, no 1, pp 18–26.

Melrose, M. and Barrett, D. (2004) *Anchors in floating lives: Interventions with young people sexually abused through prostitution*, London: Russell House Publications.

Melrose, M., Barrett, D. and Brodie, I. (1999) *One way street? Retrospectives on childhood prostitution*, London: The Children's Society.

Millie, A., Jacobson, J., MacDonald, E. and Hough, M. (2005) *Anti-social behaviour strategies: Finding a balance*, Bristol: The Policy Press for Joseph Rowntree Foundation.

Ministry of Justice (2008) *The Report of the Prostitution Law Review Committee on the Operation of the Prostitution Reform Act 2003*, Wellington, NZ: Ministry of Justice.

Mitchell, F. (2004) *Living in limbo: Survey of homeless households living in temporary accommodation*, London: Shelter.

Mitrovic, E. (2004) *Working in the sex industry: Report on the findings of a field research*, Berlin: ver.di.

Moffatt, P.G. and Peters, S.A. (2004) 'Pricing personal services: an empirical study of earnings in the UK prostitution industry', *Scottish Journal of Political Economy*, vol 51, no 5, pp 675–90.

Morrison, T. and Whitehead, B. (2007) *Male sex work: A business doing pleasure*, Binghamton: The Haworth Press.

Mouffe, C. (1995) 'Post-Marxism, democracy and identity', *Environment and Planning, Society and Space*, vol 13, no 3, pp 259–65.

Muncie, J. (2000) 'Pragmatic realism: searching for criminology in the new youth justice', in B. Goldson (ed) *The new youth justice*, Lyme Regis: Russell House Publishing.

Neale, J., Bloor, M.J., Berney, L. and Fischer, J. (2006) 'The effects of user involvement on treatment', *Druglink*, vol 21, no 1, pp 20–21, January/February.

New Zealand Press Association (2008) 'Law changes hasn't led to more prostitutes', 23 May, p 1.

Newman, J. (2003) 'New Labour, governance and the politics of diversity', in B. Dent and M. O'Neill (eds), *Gender and the public sector: Professionals and managerial change*, London: Routledge.

O'Connell Davidson, J. (1998) *Prostitution, power and freedom*, Cambridge: Polity Press.

O'Connell Davidson, J. (2003) '"Sleeping with the enemy"? Some problems with feminist abolitionist calls to penalise those who buy commercial sex', *Social Policy and Society*, vol 2, no 1, pp 55–64.

O'Connell Davidson, J. (2005) *Children in the global sex trade*, Cambridge: Polity Press.

O'Connell Davidson, J. (2006) 'Will the real sex slave please stand up?', *Feminist Review*, vol 83, no 1, pp 4–22.

O'Neill, M. (1997) 'Prostitute women now', in G. Scambler and A. Scambler (eds) *Rethinking prostitution: Purchasing sex in the 1990s*, London: Routledge.

O'Neill, M. (2001) *Prostitution and feminism: Towards a politics of feeling*, Cambridge: Polity Press.

O'Neill, M. and Campbell, R. (2006) 'Street sex work and local communities: creating discursive spaces for genuine consultation and inclusion', in R. Campbell and M. O'Neill (eds) *Sex work now*, Cullompton: Willan Publishing.

O'Neill, M., Stokes, L., Jayne, M. and Giddens, S. (2000) 'Love for sale: the politics of prostitution in Stoke', in T. Edensor (ed) *Reclaiming Stoke-on-Trent: Leisure, space and identity in the Potteries*, Staffordshire: Staffordshire University Press/Trentham Books.

O'Neill, M., Woods, P. and Webster, M. (2004) 'New arrivals: participatory action research, imagined communities and "visions" of social justice', *Journal of Social Justice*, vol 32, no 1, pp 75–89.

O'Neill, M., Campbell, R., Hubbard, P., Pitcher, J. and Scoular, J. (2008) 'Living with the other: street sex work, contingent communities and degrees of communities', *Crime, Media and Culture*, vol 4, no 1, pp 73–93.

Outshoorn, J. (ed) (2004) *The politics of prostitution: Women's movements, democratic states and the globalisation of sex commerce*, Cambridge: Cambridge University Press.

Pakulski, J. (1977) 'Cultural citizenship', *Citizenship Studies*, vol 1, pp 73–86.

Parker, H. (2004) 'The new drugs interventions industry: what outcomes can drugs/criminal justice treatment programmes realistically deliver?' *Probation Journal*, vol 51, no 4, pp 379–88.

Parker, H., Aldridge, J. and Egginton, R. (2001) *UK drugs unlimited*, Basingstoke: Palgrave.

Parsons, J.T., Koken, J.A. and Bimbi, D.S. (2007) 'Looking beyond HIV: eliciting individual and community needs of male internet escorts', in T. Morrison and B. Whitehead (eds) *Male sex work: A business doing pleasure*, Binghamton: The Haworth Press, pp 219–40.

Pearce, J. (1997) 'Selling sex, doing drugs and keeping safe', in A. Marlow and G. Pearson (eds) *Young people, drugs and community safety*, Lyme Regis: Russell House Publishing.

Pearce, J. (2006) 'Who needs to be involved in safeguarding sexually exploited young people?', *Child Abuse Review*, vol 5, no 5, pp 326–41.

Pearce, J. (2007) 'Sex and risk', in J. Coleman and A. Hagell (eds) *Adolescence, risk and resilience: Against the odds*, London: John Wiley.

Pearce, J., Williams, M. and Galvin, C. (2003) *It's someone taking a part of you: A study of sexual exploitation*, London: National Children's Bureau and the Joseph Rowntree Foundation.

Penfold, C., Hunter, G., Campbell, R. and Barham, L. (2004) 'Tackling client violence in female street prostitution: inter-agency working between outreach agencies and the police', *Policing & Society*, vol 14, no 4, pp 365–79.

Phoenix, J. (2001) *Making sense of prostitution*, London: Palgrave.

Phoenix, J. (2002) 'In the name of prostitution: youth prostitution policy reforms in England and Wales', *Critical Social Policy*, vol 22, no 2, pp 353–75.

Phoenix, J. (2003) 'Rethinking youth prostitution: national provision at the margins of child protection and youth justice', *Youth Justice*, vol 3, no 3, pp 152–68.

Phoenix, J. (2004) 'Regulating sex: young people, prostitution and policy reform', in B. Brooks-Gordon, L. Gelsthorpe, M. Johnson and A. Bainham (eds) *Sexuality repositioned*, Oxford: Hart Publishing.

Phoenix, J. and Oerton, S. (2005) *Illicit and illegal. Sex, regulation and social control*, Cullompton: Willan Publishing.

Pitcher, J. (2006) 'Support services for women working in the sex industry', in R. Campbell and M. O'Neill (eds) *Sex work now*, Cullompton: Willan Publishing.

Phoenix, J. (2008) 'Reinventing the wheel: contemporary contours of prostitution regulation' in G. Letherby, J. Williams, P. Birch, and M. Cain, *Sex as crime*, Cullompton: Willan Publishing.

Pitcher, J., Campbell, R., Hubbard, P., O'Neill, M. and Scoular, J. (2006) *Living and working in areas of street sex work: From conflict to coexistence*, Bristol: The Policy Press and Joseph Rowntree Foundation.

Pitts, J. (1997) 'Causes of prostitution, new forms of practice and political responses', in D. Barrett (ed) *Child prostitution in Britain: Dilemmas and practical responses*, London: The Children's Society.

Pitts, J. (2000) 'The new youth justice and the politics of electoral anxiety', in B. Goldson (ed) *The new youth justice*, Lyme Regis: Russell House Publishing.

Pitts, J. (2008) *Reluctant gangsters*, Cullompton: Willan Publishing.

Plant, M. (1997) 'Alcohol, drugs and social milieu', in G. Scambler and A. Scambler (eds) *Rethinking prostitution: Purchasing sex in the 1990s*, London: Routledge.

Pratt, J. (1999) 'Sex crime and the new punitiveness', Paper presented at the History of Crime, Policing and Punishment conference convened by the Australian Institute of Criminology in conjunction with Charles Stuart University, Canberra, 9–10 December.

Rhodes, R. (2000) 'The governance narrative: lessons from the Whitehall Programme', *Public Administration*, vol 78, no 2, pp 344-62.

Rice, B. (2006) *Against the odds*, London: Shelter.

Rich, G.R. and Guidroz, K. (2000) 'Smart girls who like sex: telephone sex workers', in R. Weitzer (ed) *Sex for sale: Prostitution, pornography and the sex industry*, London: Routledge.

Roberts, R., Bergström, S. and La Rooy, D. (2007) 'Commentary: UK students and sex work: current knowledge and research issues', *Journal of Community and Applied Social Psychology*, vol 17, no 1, pp 141–6.

Robinson, T. (1989) *London's homosexual male prostitutes: Power peer groups and HIV*, Project Sigma Working Papers, Southbank University, London: HMSO.

Rowlands, M. (2005) 'The state of ASBO Britain: the rise of intolerance', ECLN Essays No 9, European Civil Liberties Network, www.ecln. org/essays/essay-9.pdf

Sagar, T. (2005) 'Street watch: concept and practice, civilian participation and street prostitution control', *British Journal of Criminology*, vol 45, no 1, pp 98–112.

Sanders, T. (2004) 'The risks of street prostitution: punters, police and protesters', *Urban Studies*, vol 41, no 8, pp 1703–17.

Sanders, T. (2005) *Sex work: A risky business*, Devon: Willan Publishing.

Sanders, T. (2007) 'Becoming an ex-sex worker', *Feminist Criminology*, vol 2. no 1, pp 74–95.

Sanders, T. (2008a) 'Male sexual scripts: intimacy, sexuality and pleasure in the purchase of commercial sex', *Sociology*, vol 42, no 1, pp 400–17.

Sanders, T. (2008b) *Paying for pleasure: Men who buy sex*, Cullompton: Willan Publishing.

Sanders, T. and Campbell, R. (2007) 'Designing out violence, building in respect: violence, safety and sex work policy', *British Journal of Sociology*, vol 58, no 1, pp 1–18.

Sanders, T. and Campbell, R. (2008) 'Why hate men who pay for sex? Exploring the shift to "tackling demand" in the UK', in V. Munro and M. della Guista (eds) *Demanding sex? Critical reflections on the supply/demand dynamic in prostitution*, Aldershot: Ashgate.

Scarlet Alliance (1999) 'Unjust and counter-productive: the failure of government to protect sex workers from discrimination', www.scarletalliance.org.au

Scott, S. and Harper, Z. (2006) 'Meeting the needs of sexually exploited young people: the challenge of conducting policy relevant research' Child Abuse Review, vol 15, pp 313–25.

Scott, S. and Skidmore, P. (2006) *Reducing the risk: Barnardo's support for sexually exploited young people*, London: Barnardo's.

Scottish Executive (2004) *Being outside: Constructing a response to street prostitution. A report of the expert group on prostitution in Scotland*, Edinburgh: The Stationery Office.

Scottish Executive (2006) *Strategic framework on violence against women*, Violence Against Women Branch, Development Department, Equalities Unit, Scottish Executive, Edinburgh: The Stationery Office.

Scoular, J. (2004) 'The "subject" of prostitution: interpreting the discursive, symbolic and material position of sex/work in feminist theory', *Feminist Theory*, vol 5, no 3, pp 343–55.

Scoular, J. and O'Neill, M. (2007) 'Regulating prostitution: social inclusion, responsibilisation and the politics of prostitution reform', *British Journal of Criminology*, vol 47, no 5, pp 764–78.

Scoular, J., Pitcher, J. and Campbell, R. (2007) 'What's anti-social about sex work? The changing representation of prostitution's incivility', *Community Safety Journal*, vol 6, no 1, pp 11–17.

Scourfield, J. and Drakeford, M. (2002) 'New Labour and "the problem of men"', *Critical Social Policy*, vol 22, no 4, pp 619–40.

Seddon, T. (2006) 'Drugs, crime and social exclusion: social context and social theory in British drugs-crime research', *British Journal of Criminology*, vol 46, no 4, pp 680–703.

Self, H. (2003) *Prostitution, women and misuse of the law: The fallen daughters of Eve*, London: Frank Cass Publishers.

SEU (Social Exclusion Unit) (2004) *Tackling social exclusion: Taking stock and looking to the future*, London: Crown Publications.

Sheffield Safeguarding Children Board (2007) *Sexual exploitation service annual report 2006–2007*, Sheffield: Sheffield Local Authority.

Sheffield Safeguarding Children Board (2008) *Annual report 2007–2008*, Sheffield: Sheffield Safeguarding Children Board.

Shelter (2008) *Supporting children and families*, www.shelter.org.uk

Shildrick, T. and MacDonald, R. (2008) 'Understanding youth exclusion: critical moments, social networks and social capital', *Youth and Policy*, no 99, pp 43–55.

Sion, A. (1977) *Prostitution and the Law*, London: Faber and Faber.

Smart, C. (1989) *Feminism and the power of law*, London, New York: Routledge.

Smith, A.-M. (1998) *Laclau and Mouffe, the radical democratic imaginary*, London: Routledge.

Smith, C. (2002) 'Shiny chests and heaving G-strings: A night out with the Chippendales', *Sexualities*, vol 5, no 1, pp 67–89.

Soothill, K. and Sanders, T. (2004) 'Calling the tune? Some observations on Paying the Price: a consultation paper on prostitution', *Journal of Forensic Psychiatry and Psychology*, vol 15, no 4, pp 642–59.

Spongberg, M. (1997) *Feminizing venereal disease: The body of the prostitute in nineteenth century literature*, London: MacMillan Press.

Squires, P. (1998) 'Cops and customers: consumerism and the demand for policing services. Is the customer always right?' *Policing and Society*, vol 8, pp 171–89.

Squires, P. (ed) (2006) *Community safety: Critical perspectives on policy and practice*, Bristol: The Policy Press.

Street Reach (2007) *Annual report*, www.streetreach.org.uk.

Sullivan, R. (2001) 'The schizophrenic state: neo-liberal criminal justice', in K. Stenson and R. Sullivan (eds) *Crime, risk and justice: The politics of crime control in liberal democracies*, Cullompton: Willan Publishing.

Svanström, Y. (2006) 'Prostitution in Sweden: debates and policies 1980–2004', in G. Gangoli and N. Westmarland (eds) *International approaches to prostitution: Law and policy in Europe and Asia*, Bristol: The Policy Press.

Swan Housing Group (2006/7) *Look Again annual report 2006/7*, www. swan.org.uk.

Swann, S and Balding, V. (2002) *Safeguarding children involved in prostitution: Guidance review*, London: The Stationery Office

TAMPEP (2004) *Final report VI*, Amsterdam: Tampep International Foundation.

Taylor, A. (1993) *Women drug users: An ethnography of a female injecting community*, Oxford: Oxford University Press.

Tester, K. (1995) *The inhuman condition*, London: Routledge.

Thomas, J. (2000) 'Gay male video pornography: past, present, and future', in R. Weitzer (ed) *Sex for sale: Prostitution, pornography and the sex industry*, London: Routledge.

Treasury Office (2003) *Every Child Matters*, Cm 5860, London: The Stationery Office.

UKNSWP (UK Network of Sex Work Projects) (2008) *Keeping safe: Safety advice for sex workers in the UK*, www.uknswp.org/resources.asp, accessed 15 August 2008.

Walkowitz, J. (1980) *Prostitution and Victorian society: Women, class and the state*, Cambridge: Cambridge University Press.

Warburton, H., Turnbull, P. and Hough, M. (2005) *Occasional and controlled heroin use: Not a problem?*, York: Joseph Rowntree Foundation.

Weitzer, R. (2005) 'Flawed theory and method in studies of prostitution', *Violence Against Women*, vol 11 no 7, pp 934–49.

West, D.J. and de Villiers, B. (1992) *Male prostitution – gay sex services in London*, London: Duckworth Press.

Whowell, M. (2006) 'Who pays the price? Exploring gender and (in)visibility in sex work policy', Paper presented at UKNSWP annual conference 'Working Within and Challenging: Critical Reflections on the National Strategies?', 6 October.

Wilcox, A. and Christmann, K. (2006) 'Sex for sale: qualitative study of male sex workers', unpublished project report, Huddersfield: University of Huddersfield.

WMP (Working Men Project) (2003) *Annual report*, London: Working Men Project.

WMP (2006) *Annual review*, London: Working Men Project.

Wolfenden Committee Report (1957) *Report of the Committee on Homosexual Offences and Prostitution*, Cmnd 247, London: HMSO.

Women's Aid (2006) *Why doesn't she leave?*, www.womensaid.org.uk/domestic-violence-articles.asp?section=0001

Young, I.M. (1990) *Justice and the politics of difference*, Oxford: Princeton University Press.

Ziersch, A., Gaffney, J. and Tomlinson, D. (2000) 'STI prevention and the male sex industry in London: evaluating a pilot peer education programme', *Sexually Transmitted Infection*, vol 76, no 6, pp 447–53.

Index

A

abolitionism
  and feminism 7-8, 13, 143-4
  as policy approach 13-14, 19-20, 24,
    29, 30, 76, 164, 166-7
    confusion of violence and
      consensual sex 138-9, 140
    and future of project work 79, 165-6
    see also criminalisation; zero-
      tolerance policies
academic study of prostitution 2-3, 31
  male sex work research themes 99,
    103-6, 110
  see also research
accommodation *see* housing needs
Action Plan on Tackling Human
  Trafficking (UK) 10
age of consent 11, 12, 19
age of sex workers and policy 12, 20-1
agency *see* autonomy and agency
Agustin, L.M. 74, 80
AIDS *see* HIV/AIDS
Allen, D.M. 104
anti-social behaviour approach 26,
  29-46
  and children and young people 127
  views of community residents 34-43,
    52-4
  see also ASBOs
Armistead Project in Liverpool 106
'arrest referral' schemes 92
ASBOs (anti-social behaviour orders)
  43, 44, 91
  displacement effect 40, 41
  residents' views on use 39-41
  and zero tolerance in Edinburgh 153,
    156
Association of Chief Police Officers 67
associational justice 52
associations with prostitution 6-12
  see also metonymic associations
Australia: decriminalisation 19, 70,
  163-4
autonomy and agency of sex workers
  94, 139, 140, 143-4

B

Barnardo's 106, 127
Barrett, D. 130
BBC 10
Berney, L. 69, 70
Bernstein, E. 81
binary distinctions 13, 49
Bland, L. 49
Blunkett, David 23, 47, 163
Booth, Bramwell 126
Boynton, P. 48
Brents, B. 74
Brooks-Gordon, B. 76
brothel prostitution
  and criminalisation approach 16, 24,
    71-81
    rejection of licensing option 73-4,
      163-4
  decriminalisation approaches 19, 30,
    51, 74, 118
    approval of small-scale indoor
      arrangements 75
  good practice and management 71-2,
    73, 74, 80, 81, 116-17
  self-regulation in male sex work
    110-11, 117, 118
  and legal parameters for indoor sex
    work 68
  male sex work 110-11
  see also indoor sex work
Buchanan, J. 87, 90, 91, 92, 93
business approach 143
  male sex work 111, 115
Butler, Josephine 126

C

Cabinet Office 162-3
Campbell, N. 87
Campbell, Rosie 52-4, 59-62, 73
Carlen, P. 163
Carnwath, T. 88-9
categorical associations 6-7
Central London Action on Street
  Health (CLASH) 106
chaotic drug use 89
Chapkis, W. 7
child poverty and government policy
  128-9, 133-4